"Great Goddess, thou art every lover, and every lover art thou ..."

Greenfire is a provocative reference source for women and men interested in strengthening their relationships. This wonderful book offers bold and innovative techniques and ideas—based on ancient knowledge—to enhance your personal development and sexual awareness.

Greenfire invites you on a journey of ecstasy with the Goddess and her consort. You will travel the yearly cycle of the Sun, experiencing the eight Sabbats, each connected to a different aspect of the Goddess and her partner. Through erotic guided fantasy, you will explore the concept of "Greenfire"—the oneness of woman and man as represented by the sexual union of the Goddess and her consort.

Contacting your divine nature through sexual expression deepens your sense of personal awareness and your connection with your lover and the Goddess. Sexual exploration in a spiritual context can even provide a bridge between the manifest and the unmanifest. When you and your partner achieve oneness with the Goddess and her consort while making love, you begin to lift the veils that distort your everyday perceptions of life, sexuality, and spirituality, and you open the door to boundless magical possibilities.

The perfect love of the Goddess and the perfect peace of the God exist within each one of us—and they can be experienced and enjoyed, given the knowledge. *Greenfire* celebrates the intimate joining of woman and man—and the ultimate sexual satisfaction and oneness their union can achieve through the power of the divine light inside themselves.

About the Author

For nearly twenty years, Sirona Knight has been studying psychology, folklore, and religion with a personal interest in goddess tradition. She has traveled to Europe, Mexico, the Pacific Northwest, and Alaska on her quest for knowledge of the goddess. She is a published poet, writer, teacher, hypnotherapist, and lecturer and holds a master's degree in psychology and leisure studies from California State University. Knight has been a student, teacher, and High Priestess of the Celtic Gywddonic Druidic tradition for many years. She has made radio and television appearances in Northern California, has been an active workshop leader for several years, and has created a series of guided imagery self-help tapes. She now lives in the Sierra Foothills with her husband and their son, two dogs, and two cats. Her writing room is situated next to an ancient Native American site, where she devotes her time to her art and craft and to enjoying life, moment by moment.

To Write to the Author

If you wish to contact the author or would like more information about this book, please write to her in care of Llewellyn Worldwide, and we will forward your request. Both the author and the publisher appreciate hearing from you and learning of your enjoyment of this book and how it has helped you. Llewellyn Worldwide cannot guarantee that every letter written to the authors can be answered, but all will be forwarded. Please write to:

Sirona Knight
% Llewellyn Worldwide
P.O. Box 64383-K386, St. Paul, MN 55164-0383, U.S.A.
Please enclose a self-addressed, stamped envelope or $1.00 to cover costs.
If outside the U.S.A., enclose international postal reply coupon.

Free Catalog from Llewellyn

For more than 90 years Llewellyn has brought its readers knowledge in the fields of metaphysics and human potential. Learn about the newest books in spiritual guidance, natural healing, astrology, occult philosophy and more. Enjoy book reviews, new age articles, a calendar of events, plus current advertised products and services. To get your free copy of *Llewellyn's New Worlds of Mind and Spirit*, send your name and address to:

Llewellyn's New Worlds of Mind and Spirit
P.O. Box 64383-K386, St. Paul, MN 55164-0383, U.S.A.

❧ GREENFIRE ❧

Making Love With the Goddess

Sirona Knight

1995
Llewellyn Publications
St. Paul, MN 55164-0383, U.S.A.

FIRST EDITION
First Printing, 1995

Cover Painting: Moon Deer
Cover Design: Linda Norton, Anne Marie Garrison
Illustrations: Lisa Hunt
Book Design, Layout, and Editing: Pamela Henkel

Library of Congress Cataloging-in-Publication Data
Knight, Sirona, 1955—
       Greenfire : making love with the goddess / Sirona Knight.
              p.   cm.
       Includes bibliographical references and index.
       ISBN 1-56718-386-7
       1. Sex—Religious aspects. 2. Goddess religion. 3. Sexual intercourse. I. Title.
       BL460.K65   1995
       299—dc20   94-25214
                                                         CIP

Printed in the United States of America

Llewellyn Publications
A Division of Llewellyn Worldwide, Ltd.
P.O. Box 64383, St. Paul, MN 55164-0383

❧ Dedication ❧

To Michael, my spiritual partner,
and to my bright son, Skylor,
for their ever-growing
ever-lasting
love, light, and laughter.

❧ Forthcoming book ☙

Moonflower: Erotic Dreaming with the Goddess

ꙮ Acknowledgements ꙮ

To oneness—the divine love of the goddesses and gods of light—for guiding me to spiritual ecstasy. A heartfelt thanks to my students and teachers on all dimensions, especially to my dear friend Marcel Vogel for reminding me to look for the implications in all things.

To my Mother and Father, and my entire family and friends everywhere, thank you for your open-mindedness, support, and loving kindness. And bright blessings and deep thanks to Nancy Mostad for making it possible for me to live my dream and to Nan Skovran for all of her help and humor.

I would like to respectfully thank D.J. Conway for her wisdom and friendship, and Lisa Hunt and Moon Deer for bringing my words to life only as true artists can. A special thanks to my editor, Pamela Henkel, for her keen eye and interest, and to Andrea Godwin for opening doors to new and exciting possibilities.

❧ Contents ❧

 Introduction

Woman holds the power
Man wields the light
Together they become
One again.

ॐ Introduction ॐ

Petals of white light begin opening, sending erotic sensations throughout her body. Blossoms of ecstasy open
inside her, filling her with expectation and desire. She
merges with shimmering waves of Greenfire, sending her
to the place where falcons fly high above the clouds. For a
few moments, he becomes every man she has ever desired.
When they make love, she becomes the goddess, and he,
her willing consort. Each feeling and sensation they experience lifts another veil of awareness, until gradually there
is no separation, only complete union.

When people become aware of the earth's cycle, they
realize the importance of renewal and creation. The goddess, or female aspect of life, becomes the embodiment of
the earth's fertility and the constant rebirth of the cycle of
life. Sexual expression figures predominately in this
renewal and re-creation of life.

The mating of female and male energies is the basis of
life. Celtic Gwyddonic tradition speaks of the perfect love
of the goddess and the perfect peace of the god, and how
these concepts exist innately within each one of us. By
using the information in the following chapters, you can
move toward this perfect union. Travel down this sensual
avenue, and achieve complete harmony with your sexuality and the ultimate bond to oneness.

Greenfire symbolizes the oneness of woman and man,
represented by the goddess and her consort. The goddess
gives us the greening of the cycle, as well as the fire of life.
The male consort represents this fire and vital force.
Mated together as Greenfire, they ride in a golden chariot

with the sun, and with the moon in a crystal ship of starlight. Together woman and man embrace in intimate harmony. Their union brings sexual satisfaction and the continued renewal of life.

Ancient Celtic people honored the never-ending cycle of the goddess and her consort through rituals performed on the eight Great Days. The ancients passed down these rituals in oral tradition. *Greenfire* uses Welsh Gwyddonic tradition, derived from the Old Tribes of Britain. In the eighteenth century, these rituals were translated into English. The Old Tribes, conquered by the iron-carrying Celts, called their religion and philosophy Gwyddoniaid.

Gwydonnic tradition bases its ritual and teachings on the concept of oneness. All becomes one. When you merge with oneness, you begin to lift the veils that distort your everyday perceptions of life, sexuality, and spirituality. Oneness is a state of mind and a way of being. Sexual union becomes a pleasurable mode for intensifying your connection to oneness.

The guided journeys in *Greenfire* beckon you and your partner to make love with the goddess and her consort, sending your bodies, minds, and spirits to new heights. Blending sexual fantasy and traditional Celtic Gwyddonic ritual and symbolism, each journey features a different aspect of the goddess and her consort. In the spring on Beltane, the goddess Belisana, the sun maiden, cavorts with her consort, the lusty Tarvos. In the fall on Samhain, the goddess Morrigan, akin to the Queen of Death, embraces her consort Dagda, the Great Father.

This book offers magical tools for personal development and growth. These tools assist you in gaining freedom and finding personal meaning through self-exploration and understanding. It becomes a process of moving from being directed by others, to being self-directed. You begin to listen to your inner voice. You merge with oneness, and pattern for the lifestyle you truly desire.

As you turn your mind to oneness, you become more aware of the energetic nature of life. Kirlian photography clearly shows an energetic field surrounding and connecting all things into one. You can learn to direct and influence this energy. The goddess and her consort represent the positive, neutral, and negative polarities of this life force. Positivity engenders positivity and creates patterns. Love symbolizes positive energy. Energy and light are by-products of positive and loving participation, acting as useful tools in all magical works. Negativity breaks patterns, disrupting the flow of energy. Understanding negativity is necessary, but the wise practitioner uses positivity, rather than negativity, in magical patterning.

When you focus all of your attention and efforts toward positive love-making, you allow yourself to express your divine nature. You become one with the goddess and her consort. Romantic sexual exploration serves as a mode to generate vast amounts of energy that can be applied to patterns you create through your expectations, desire, and rapport with oneness. Making love uses feelings and emotions like threads to weave patterns specified by you and your partner. These patterns or creations, like children, become a sacred tapestry representing your union.

Experiencing pleasure and satisfaction in love-making gives you an opportunity to increase your knowledge and skills. As you become more comfortable with the nature of sexual energy, you develop faith in your essential self, becoming aware of deeper subtleties and innate personal abilities. Sexual union is a way of re-creating the universe, and reflects a desire for kinship and immortality. During orgasm, your totality of being participates in an ancient sacred rite of personal transformation.

Sexual exploration is a matter of individual choice. Gwyddonic tradition teaches the importance of self-honesty

5

and self-responsibility in personal choice. You are unique. Because of this, each sexual experience becomes an original adventure and an intimate discovery with your partner and within yourself. Sharing sexual fantasies, learning one another's sexual preferences, and understanding each other's attitudes toward sexual expression all contribute toward a positive and fulfilling relationship.

You create and shape your relationships with others. Factors such as initial attraction, friendship, sexual compatibility, common interests, and spiritual compatibility contribute in the evolution of your relationship with your mate. You might desire your lover to be active, passionate, artistic, and adventuresome. Whatever the relationship you choose, merging with the goddess and her consort, while making love, links you to the boundless and the infinite magical possibilities therein.

Sexual exploration, using ancient knowledge and ritual, provides a bridge between the manifest and the unmanifest. Making love moves you to a magical place where time and space change and you flow beyond the routine world of logic and fact. Earthly reality becomes transient, and the mind prepares to accept the incredible and unknown—to be free, unfettered, and divine.

You actively shape your future. Remembering your divine nature through sexual expression deepens your sense of personal awareness and reality. This deeper awareness reacquaints you with the never-ending, ever-changing cycle of the goddess and her consort. Reach out with your mind now, and dance with effortless grace through the seasons, along the eight Great Days following the path of the sun. The universe, full of magic, eagerly waits for our minds to grow sharper. Allow yourself to rediscover the magical oneness of life, and do whatever most arouses you to love.

CHAPTER ONE

❧ Yule ❧

Kerridwen & Kernunnos

Greenfire
So soft as you move with her
Wondrous, enchanting, all brilliance
As she beckons you with gesture and flame.

❧ Yule ❧

Kerridwen & Kernunnos

The element is earth

The Goddess and Her Consort

She who is the mother of all things issued out of that which is nameless. The All Mother wished to create a balance and harmony of all energies and so she created a mate, a reflection of herself. She called him the All Father. Every aspect or quality of the goddess has a male counterpart referred to as the consort.

The goddess anchored her mate's nature, like her own, to the seasons and the cycles so that after Yule, his bright nature would begin to awaken and would be strong and vital on the Spring Equinox. His bright nature rules the complete cycle or season of the greening. With the harvest comes the time for the consort's dark nature to rule and roam the land while his bright nature enters winter sleep.

The eight high days of power remind us of the consort's progress through the seasons. The role of the Great Moons and the Great Days is to tune oneself to these recurring cycles, increasing awareness of one's environment, internal tides, and personal cycles. The ancient Gywdonnic druids were well aware of the knowledge held within nature's grasp, and they based their timekeeping method on the observation of the sun and the moon.

From the moon's cycles, the druids devised a calendar that was comprised of twelve half-months of fifteen nights each, and twelve half-months of fourteen nights each. This left three and one-quarter nights remaining each year. These odd nights were inserted into their calendar, and depending upon placement and circumstances, were considered to be especially lucky or unlucky. Similarly, certain other nights throughout the year were thought to be either fortunate or unpropitious. Transition points, keying in to the waxing and waning patterns of the moon, were considered significant times of power.

The druids observed that the solar year seemed to naturally divide into eight equal portions. They distinguished the solstice and equinox points as four Great Days. Another four Great Days were carefully calculated halfway between each of the first four, so that every forty-five days, one of the Great Days was celebrated.

Using their ability to predict seasons and cycles through very exacting methods, the druids had the advantage of knowing the proper times to plant, breed, and harvest. This knowledge enhanced their peoples' survival rate and lifestyle.

The sun and the moon played significant parts in ancient times, as they still do today. The modern practitioner may have noticed that the order of the Great Days corresponds to the path of the sun. In Gwydonnic tradition, the first dawning of spring occurs on the Great Day of Bridget's Fire. The spring season moves from Bridget's Fire to Beltane. Summer embraces Beltane in an adventure of the sun, cycling into Lughnassad. Autumn moves from Lughnassad to Samhain; and the winter cycle starts at Samhain and flows into Bridget's Fire.

Today, calculating the Great Days is simple. Using an ephemeris, you can find the exact date based on eight equal divisions of the solar year as designated in tropical astrology. Use the following parameters in your calculations (also see Chart on Page 195):

Yule/Winter Solstice at 00.00 degrees Capricorn

Bridget's Fire at 15.00 degrees Aquarius

Hertha's Day/Spring Equinox at 00.00 degrees Aries

Beltane at 15.00 degrees Taurus

Letha's Day/Summer Solstice at 00.00 degrees Cancer

Lughnassad at 15.00 degrees Leo

Hellith's Day/Autumnal Equinox at 00.00 degrees Libra

Samhain at 15.00 degrees Scorpio

The eight Great Days are symbols of the seasons and the spirit. This concept extended into the culture and politics of the ancient people of the British Isles. Divisions of four represented the sacred renewal patterns of their world. Ireland, for example, was divided into four kingdoms with the High King's sector situated in the center of the four. Britain was partitioned in a similar pattern. Traditionally, the four queens from each of these kingdoms made love with the High King, as it was his sacred duty and their sacred trust. Literally and figuratively, each of the four queens was viewed as a goddess on earth.

The legend of King Arthur depicts the basic principles of this ancient custom. It was Uther Pendragon's sacred right to make love with Igraine, Arthur's mother, who was married to the understandably uncooperative and resistant Duke of Cornwall. This may well have played a part in the war between Pendragon and the Duke. Uther could not claim his rightful title as High King until he had fulfilled his duty and bedded each of the four Great Queens.

Representing the elements, the four Great Queens held the seasons and land in balance. Igraine, for example, means "she of the sun," and she was the queen of the southern kingdom. The South point represents the element fire which suggests that queen Igraine was the embodiment of the sun goddess Bridget on earth. Keeping in step with the four natural divisions of the path of the sun, the three other Great Queens were: Morgan Le Fay, queen of the west and the element water, who was an embodiment of the goddess Morgana; Margawse, the northern queen representing the element earth, who was human counterpart to the goddess Morrigu; and Elayne, the queen of the east and the element air, who was identified with the goddess Viviana.

The goddess and her consort, dancing in a never-ending, ever-changing rhythm through the solar year, weave the pattern called light. The eight Great Days are times for you to don this fabric woven by the goddess and her mate, fashioned in whatever costume you choose. Symbolically dressed for the part, you then begin your journey through the eyes of the goddess.

Yule is the first Great Day. The ritual begins slightly before midnight and ends shortly after midnight. This Great Day is traditionally celebrated on the eve of the Winter Solstice, and parallels the Mithraic observance of the birth of the sun. Yule ritual honors the lengthening of the day with the return of the sun. Our bright lord rises out of the dust from his winter sleep. The golden bull, Tarvos, is reborn and returns to the land. His divine light shines once again on the earth for the goddess has heard the plea and returns the consort to the land.

The symbolic rebirth of Tarvos is represented by a lighted live evergreen tree. The tree is decorated with candles. Three women, representing the Threefold goddess, light the candles with concentrated care. After the ritual, the live tree is then planted in an optimal spot.

Other festivities on Yule include the burning of the Yule log. In parts of Northern Europe, people believe that a piece of the Yule log, if kept safe during the year, will protect the house, give the safekeepers a bountiful harvest, and help the livestock give birth easily. Hanging mistletoe and spreading holly branches on the mantel are also practices thought to bring luck with fertility.

Yule is a time to examine your inner self. Forgiveness of yourself and others is encouraged on this Great Day. All negative feelings can be shed. Customarily, you can write down one thing you would most like to eliminate in your life. Rip the paper into small pieces and burn it in the Yule fire with the expectation and intention of ridding yourself of the designated burden.

Yule brings with it the hope that you can learn from your experiences over the previous year, and that this wisdom will create more positive patterns in your life. Gifts are exchanged as symbols of love and renewal. At the end of the ritual, it is traditional to dance a circle dance while calling out the names of the goddess and god, chanting the names over and over, louder and faster: "Ker-rid-wen, Ker-nun-nos!"

The energy and merriment continue during the feast and throughout the evening. The All Mother, the goddess Kerridwen, and the All Father, the consort Kernunnos, preside over the Yule festivities. Kerridwen depicts the goddess of inspiration and knowledge referred to as the Ninefold One. She looks diaphanous, like pale moonlight, and her magical tool is a large cauldron. Kernunnos symbolizes the lord of the animals. He represents the lord of life and death, and of wealth. He wears a serpent belt and animal horns on his head. His curly brown hair is thick.

He has earthy features that can be ruddy or fair, and brown or hazel eyes. His symbols are a stag, a bull, three cranes, a rat, and a bag of flowing coins.

The bright face of Kerridwen always is positive. She appears as pure white light, or she can seem like a white fog or pale moonlight. She feels all pervasive, and seems to be everywhere, in all things at all times. Kerridwen acts very protective and mother-like. She can be any age, ancient or young, but usually appears to be 35 or older. She embodies the All Mother—all reproduction and creation in nature. The manifest universe arises from her magical cauldron.

The goddess Kerridwen grants wishes when you have a strong and clear enough desire. With a thought, she transforms the universe. With a breath, she can cause the winds to blow or to be silent. With a touch, she creates mountains, valleys, forests, oceans, and rivers.

When Kerridwen looks upon you, you transform. She becomes total radiance, balance, perfect love, and more. When she walks or moves, it is as if she is gracefully floating. Her face seems in constant motion. Her long hair appears white, and her eyes look golden green or like pure brilliant light. She feels strong and powerful, and is always gentle.

Her consort Kernunnos represents all men. He depicts all male energy in nature, all power, and he has great strength. Large in stature and very muscular, each of his muscles is well defined, as if it is used often. There is nothing in excess about him, nothing wasted. His serpent belt acts as his companion and as a source of never-ending knowledge.

Kernunnos is reborn each year with the seasons. He portrays the king of the forest, the fields, and lover of all women. His skin feels rough to the touch and his hands are worn and calloused. He often has a day or two's growth of whiskers or a full beard. His chin is square and his eyes gleam large, like those of a deer. His features are strong and his face has well-defined wrinkles. He appears young at times, tough and rowdy. At other times he seems ancient, quietly strong and wise.

The consort has a great deal of initiating energy. Kernunnos shows you how to begin patterns and then he fertilizes the seeds. He is honored and obeyed.

Intense sexual experiences can be shared with Kernunnos as he appears very well endowed.

Yule is the time of year when the All Mother and the All Father arise out of oneness. The light is reborn and beginning to grow. The goddess Kerridwen and her consort Kernunnos represent the potential for creation, growth, love, and wisdom. How you, the practitioner, choose to use these Yuletide gifts, is completely up to you.

Practical Knowledge and Useful Instruction— Setting Up Stone and Crystal Grids

The light is reborn; the energy renewed. But what is this energy? Everything is made up of energy and has an energetic field surrounding it. In living things, this field is more pronounced and varies depending upon the physical, emotional, and spiritual characteristics of the entity. In essence, we are all light beings who absorb and emanate energy fields that extend beyond our being. Spirit, mind, and body become vehicles for this energy.

One way to learn the properties of energy fields and light is to become familiar with the uses of stones and crystals. The major premise of this work is that everything is energy. Thought becomes energy. Intention becomes energy. Energy manifests into form, and form becomes reality. In other words, you can pattern energy by using stones and crystals in certain ways. Crystals and gemstones, like our minds, amplify energy and can be used to intensify and direct experience. Utilizing the stones helps to balance and focus this energy.

Experiment with your stones. Learn to trust your intuition as to the methods that work for you. Basic information on stones and crystals is available in several interesting books, audio tapes, and video tapes. Knowledgeable shop keepers and local practitioners can also be excellent sources of information.

While learning more about crystal and stone lore, begin to explore the ways you can use this knowledge to pattern energy. One effective method uses a crystal grid with intention, breath work, and progressive relaxation. This creates a relaxed and receptive state of awareness.

A grid is a group of stones linked together to form an energy field. You can use grids in various ways, ranging from enhancing your sexual experience to ridding yourself of negative energy in your home or work place. Potential uses of grids are limitless, and merely depend upon your imagination, desire, and effort.

Grids are based on the principles of ley lines. Ley lines are invisible lines of power that crisscross the countryside. The term "lay of the land" comes from the awareness of these lines of energy. Originally they were used as thoroughfares, trackways, and sources of power. Early people harnessed this power by erecting places of worship such as henges, temples, and churches at certain points along the ley lines. Natural formations such as wells, rivers, and rock outcroppings are often situated on ley lines.

Constructing a grid creates a unified energy field very akin to a ley line. This causes an energy vortex which produces higher vibrations of light. Grids serve as communication links with this energy and power. When you form a grid, you are creating an energetic pattern. With this pattern, you can weave light and manifest your reality.

An even stronger energetic field can be created when you program the stones within a grid. This more intense power can be generated for magic and high magic depending upon your intention.

First, clear your stones. Then carefully visualize in your mind how the grid will be used and for what purpose and pattern. Merge with the stones and move your mind energy into them. Become the stones; take on the qualities you have imbued in them.

A common grid formation consists of eight clear crystal points placed around the body; one at the head, one at the feet, and two each at the shoulders, hips, and knees. When the stones are pointed in, whatever is inside the grid receives or absorbs energy. If the crystals are pointed out, the energy from the grid emits outward into the manifest world and beyond.

17

Another powerful grid pattern is the pentagram. Clear crystal points are placed around the head, hands, and feet of the person inside the grid. To intensify or build upon the energy of the pentagram grid, position the gemstones over the seven basic chakra areas. This pattern will induce an even deeper magical state of merging and insight when each chakra is played with its corresponding musical tone. Because sound and our bodies are both comprised of wave forms, they interrelate and affect one another.

Start at the crown chakra and work down the center of the body, placing clear quartz or lapis at the crown. Play a B note. Cover the third eye with tourmaline, herkimer, clear quartz, garnet, or moonstone, sounding an A note. Use a blue stone on the throat area while you play a G note. Green or pink stones work well on the heart chakra, which harmonizes with an F note. Moving down, place rutilated quartz, citrine, clear quartz, or tourmaline on the solar plexus while playing an E note. Try carnelian, agate, jasper, or cats eye on the second chakra and use a D note. Finish with hematite, black tourmaline, or obsidian on the survival chakra, while playing a C note. Also try moving in the opposite direction, up the chakras and musical scale.

When working with another person inside grids, ask how each stone feels on his or her body. Suggest that your partner close his or her eyes and breathe deeply and completely. Connect the stones that are positioned on the chakras with the stones around the body. Use your mind's energy in a clockwise motion, visualizing a white or golden thread connecting the stones. This strengthens the effect of the grid.

Use mental imagery and positive suggestion to assist your partner in merging with the energy of the grid. Often experiences in a grid seem more intense and powerful. A deeper feeling of relaxation and peaceful awareness comes into play, as though you were actually in the experience, realm, or dimension. In other words, work with the suggestions by using your mind's energy, as if you were living a story. The more involved you become in the process and participation of building up the magical experience, the better the results.

After sufficient time has elapsed, remove the stones starting at the crown chakra or third eye, generally in the same way you put them on. While working within the grid, be sure to tell your partner what you are doing: "I'm removing the stones now." He or she will be able to notice shifts of energy in the grid when you move in and out of the grid or reposition stones; these shifts can startle your partner.

The more you practice with stones and crystals, the better the experience. The deeper you merge with oneness, the easier it is to let go and throw yourself wholeheartedly into the experience. Have fun and create your own personal adventure with the stones and grids. Each experience will differ and will add to your awareness and ability. Use every experience to gain knowledge. Tailor the suggestions on grids to fit into your personal life- style. Using your own words and images, allow your imagination to freely roam and explore.

When you engage in imagining, daydreaming, or fantasizing, you construct hypothetical situations and make-believe roles, visualizing how you might act in a particular event. It is wise to learn to do this privately rather than publicly.

The ritual use of crystals and stones in grid work and healing goes beyond one's imagination—far beyond fantasy, into the magical world of boundless possibilities. A deep well of knowledge within each of us waits to arise and assist us in our adventure of life. We can learn to merge with this knowledge. Using intention and desire, we can truly see our existences through the eyes of the goddess and her consort.

19

Let us take this journey and live the stories together. For each individual, the experience will be unique. Remember to use the energy you create, and to pattern wisely. Allow the pleasure of living and loving into your life as you travel with the goddess and her consort through each of the eight Great Days, beginning with Yule.

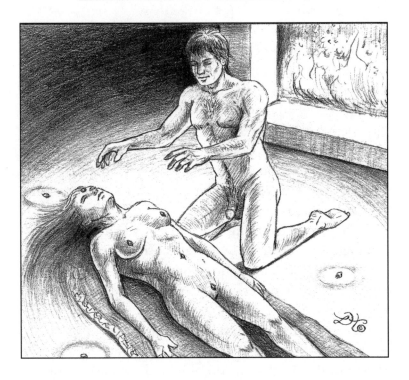

Guided Journey: Yule

The rain outside taps in the night against the walls of the house. Inside, she lays naked, her porcelain skin translucent as a pearl on the emerald green quilt. Red embroidered holly berries cover the quilt's edges. Her long silken hair spreads out against the emerald expanse and fans out into a beautiful weave, blending with the embroidery. The quilt is velvety and warm against her smooth skin.

Moonlight cascades through the window, illuminating the room and making her skin glow as she lies quietly in the crystal grid. Eight clear crystals, all pointing inward, are strategically positioned in a circle surrounding her.

Each facet echoes the light of the moon, activating the grid with a stream of light and encircling her body like delicately shaped flames. The petals of light connect her to the energy from which all life stems—to oneness.

She also becomes aware of the seven chakra stones that caress her naked torso with beads of light. All of her chakras vibrate in harmony like the delicately plucked strings of a harp; each voice an integral part in a symphony.

Her senses begin to expand as the energy of the stones on her body meld with the flames of the crystal grid. She feels feathers as her arms become wings and she begins to float on a bed of air. She floats gently to the ceiling, then beyond the room as her senses continue to expand.

She feels a breeze on her cheek, and becomes aware of the turbulence all about her. The tops of trees dance with a fury that knows no bounds. With a deep breath, she realizes no winter storm can penetrate her shield of light. Letting her mind travel out further, she senses an oasis of tranquility, a beacon of light within the boundlessness of a hurricane.

She descends through the clouds that stretch out like giant balls of cotton floating gently upward, giving way to a deserted beach. As she touches the sand, ocean waves caress her naked flesh with a tingling sensation that begins at her toes and ripples up to her head until it engulfs her entire body. The sand is warm and sensual as she buries herself deeper within its cocoon. Her wings return to arms.

Through the splashing of the waves, she hears the footsteps of her lover, approaching ever closer, until she smells the odor of his sweat beading up in the hot sun. By the sound of his footsteps, she knows that he stands directly in front of her.

She opens her eyes and watches as he lights two candles, one green for the goddess and one red for the god. He picks up the incense burner and lights the mixture. A light cloud of smoke moves her way. She takes a deep breath. The smell of frankincense and myrrh brings her slowly and gradually back into the room, into the crystal grid.

Her awareness continues to expand as she watches her lover prepare for Yule. After lighting the Yule tree, he stacks the wood in the fireplace, moving each piece with care and precision. He draws the match to the kindling, and the small pieces ignite in flame. The smell of pine mingles with the incense. Soon the fire roars in passion, the flames spreading out like the petals of a flower.

Her lover turns toward her and she sees him for the first time, his naked skin gleaming in the glow of the firelight. Sleek as a mountain lion, his every muscle looks well defined, part of a greater pattern. She sees him as all men and all lovers. He sees her as all women and all lovers. She is white light, primal energy. Together they are the All Mother and the All Father mating once again, balancing the seasons in the continual rebirth.

He asks quietly to step inside the grid, and she beckons him with a smile of light. He steps inside and slowly kneels beside her. He removes the amethyst stone from her crown chakra. She feels the heat emanating from his hand as it gently massages the top of her head, sweeping her hair back and weaving its lush silkiness through his fingers.

While removing the citrine from her third eye, he rubs amber-scented oil into her skin using clockwise motions. His finger feels warm as it draws circles around her consciousness. Her awareness continues to expand and she becomes more and more aware of his presence, of his maleness.

From her throat chakra, he removes a round flat piece of malachite. She looks into his eyes, and they lock into an animal stare. She feels wild and uncontrollable, yet cuddly and soft.

Plucking garnets from her breasts, he nibbles at her nipples, glistening in the firelight. He pours droplets of the richly-scented oil on her throat and gradually begins spreading them down across her breasts. His hands sensually heat her with every stroke.

He lifts the diamond from her solar plexus. She feels his oily fingers as they caress her with clockwise circles which begin small, but soon encompass the vast expanse of the universe. She feels the strength of his rippling muscles, his desire, his intent.

He moves his mouth down to her stomach. His teeth bite down and remove the ruby from her navel. His tongue plunges into her belly button, creating magical circles that move out into infinity. She feels the hot moistness of his mouth as he softly licks her skin.

Gently plucking the tourmaline, he kisses every petal of her flower. She softly moans, darting her fingers through his hair as his head bobs back and forth. They both feel the intertwining until they are one. Ecstasy heightens with her every heartbeat, pounding louder and louder.

His mouth begins the long laborious journey to her mouth. Through valleys and mountains, her body trembles and quakes until at last lips meet lips, and bodies embrace with a quiver of anticipation. The energy of the crystal grid intensifies the waves of passion between them. The power feels mighty, like a volcano, with each eruption more magnificent than the one before it.

He moves between her silken legs and she feels him inside of her, filling her, stroking her with his desire. He feels all powerful, with incredible endurance and stamina. He seems like a an animal, a bull or a bear, when he moves into her. He wants to move into her harder and harder, and groans in appreciation when she encourages him and coaxes him deeper. He plunges and pushes himself further into her with every motion, every moment.

He moves into her like waves of shimmering white light, waves that keep breaking inside of her, hot waves. She feels completely dominated, filled, and satiated. For a few moments, he is every man she has ever wanted to make love to, every man she has ever desired inside of her, like being communally loved by all the men in her deepest and most secret fantasies.

She surrounds him with her desire, with her light. He seems to grow harder and longer as they make love, enlarging with each powerful thrust.

She feels the liquid fire as they join as one, goddess and god. Hot chills race down her body and back up again. He moves out of her, and she notices he is still hard and firm as if he could make love with her forever and a day.

As they gaze into each other's eyes, the reflection of the fire moves with them into oneness. The sweat from their bodies flows like two rivers into one.

 Bridget's Fire

Bridget & Belenus

My mind moves out from behind my eyes
To places yet unvisited by the voyager
Shards of another reality
Gods make the best tour guides
They know all the hot spots.

ᔐ Bridget's Fire ᔐ

Bridget & Belenus

Element is halfway between earth and air

The Goddess and Her Consort

Traveling along the path of the sun after Yule, the Great Day of Bridget's Fire (also called Imbolc or Oiemelc) falls at the beginning of February. On this Great Day we honor the sun goddess Bridget, who represents fire of fire. She acts as the patroness of hearth and home, of poets and artisans, and of smiths and craftsmen. Her name means "bright one."

Fire was not only essential to the livelihood of ancient people, but its sacredness also figured predominately in their spiritual lives. Long ago, Bridget's temple served as the sanctuary of a sacred fire which supplied the elemental fire of the sun. This fire was never allowed to burn out except once each year on the eve of Bridget's Fire. On the morning of the Great Day, the High Priestess who symbolized the goddess herself lit a new fire out of nine carefully selected types of wood. This newly ignited fire was called the need fire.

Throughout the countryside, every household let their fires die out on Bridget's Eve. The next day, women went to the temple seeking the sacred fire. They would each light a branch from the fire, and carry it home to start their own hearth fires. Lighting the fire, they would chant to the goddess, "Bridget, Bridget, Bridget, brightest flame. Bridget, Bridget, Bridget, sacred name!" If the home fires died at any time other than the eve of Bridget's Fire, it was considered an unfavorable omen.

Tradition of this Great Day states that a fruit tree be planted as an embodiment of the goddess. Bridget represents the earth's fertility.

In the British Isles, on the Isle of Man, customarily the head of the household asks a family member to wait outside the front door holding a potted fruit tree. Those inside the house call out together, "Bridget, Bridget, come to my house, come to my house tonight. Open the door for Bridget, and let Bridget come in."

The member waiting outside the door then knocks loudly three times. The door is solemnly opened and the tree is brought inside and treated like royalty for the evening. The next morning, on Bridget's Fire, they plant the tree.

As the fertility and fire goddess, Bridget carries a firepot symbolizing the cauldron, a spindle, and a distaff— her magical tools. Bridget acts as the Triple Goddess, portraying complementary aspects of the sun, earth, and moon within one figure. Her symbol is fire, and she is called the Bright Arrow. She governs smithcraft, inspiration, and healing, and typifies the strong and intense feminine force of fertility. As the daughter of the Dagda, the Good God, Bridget represents all wisdom. Her ancient name, Brigantia, means "bride." She is also credited for bringing whistling to humankind on a night when she wanted to call to her consort, Belenus, and her friends.

Belenus, a god of truth, inspiration, life and music, also symbolizes fire of fire. As a young man, he represents the male aspect of the sacred flame. Belenus carries a sun disc, a golden sword, a spear, and plays a harp made of gold. He is an aspect of the ancient god Bel, and a god of the earth and consort to the Lady.

Together Bridget and her consort Belenus welcome the dawn and sunrise. They are akin to the Greek gods Venus and Apollo. They embody the divine qualities of brightness and wisdom, and bring the light of the sacred flame and sun. The goddess and her consort walk across sunbeams in the morning. They represent the need fire for one another. Bridget and Belenus offer courage, strength, and renewed desire. She acts as bride to Belenus and to every man—the match to the flame. She portrays bride energy and all the joy that being a bride entails.

Bridget feels like spring, like fields of grass warming in the morning sun. She smells of honeysuckle and lilacs. Depicted as a young woman with long golden hair, her eyes are piercing, bright white light; they appear as all colors. She wears golden-hued or white robes. As the shining goddess, Bridget shows love for all nature, especially animals. She symbolizes the initial flame, a strong female energy that can be effectively directed.

Belenus acts as her perfect mate. His skin is hot, glowing, and bright. His touch feels like the caress of a healing fire. He is consuming like the flame, yet he never burns those he touches. The consort's energy is penetrating, like a shaft of sunlight or a laser beam.

The consort Belenus emits the spicy scent of the forest. He appears with blonde or light hair, and has a tall, lean, and athletic body. He moves quickly and directly. He wears light blue, gold, and white robes, but often appears nude with an even suntan. The consort's eyes are light blue. His face is well defined, with prominent cheekbones and a strong chin. He is clean shaven, and has a high fore-head and finely-chiseled mouth.

Belenus, like Bridget, is sensual and sexual. As sym-bols of fire, the goddess and her consort give those who honor them a great deal of energy to work magical pat-terns. Bridget's energy is concentrated, fertile, and stimu-lating. Belenus' energy is potent and dynamic.

The sun goddess and her consort are excellent gods to merge with to create patterns in your life. Bring in the divine qualities of Bridget to foretell events. In doing so, your magical patterns will take on new proportions and expanded depth. Improve your abilities to manifest and create as you merge with Belenus.

When you take on the characteristics of the goddess and her consort, you seek your inner flame. Your mind moves beyond itself and integrates the aspects of Bridget and Belenus within you by merging with oneness.

Practical Knowledge and Useful Instruction— Oneness and Merging

The premise of oneness revolves around the concept that all things, living and otherwise, are one boundless being. Each aspect of oneness is both truly unique and part of the commonality. The goddess and her consort represent oneness, and they live in the boundless. By embracing the concept of oneness, you can open new doors to under-standing and self-development. Comprehending oneness is more easily grasped by the creative right side of your brain, which readily understands concepts and symbols.

Knowing oneness is a personal choice and the ideal avenue for self-discovery. Move beyond the limitations imposed upon you by your mind. The capabilities of the mind surpass your present conceptions.

Moment by moment, knowing oneness can improve your proficiency in magic and just about everything else. The formula for knowing oneness, and for that matter, creating any pattern in magic, comprises three basic steps:
- expectation
- desire
- merging

The probable success of all magical work depends upon the clarity of your expectation, the strength of your desire, and the depth of your merge.

The most effective method for building your relationship with oneness is through a process called merging, which allows you to reach a level of synchronicity with all things—the boundless and the ground of being. This uncharted potential of mind and moving mind can be tapped through this process. By merging, you can experience oneness firsthand, storing the information and building your life pattern with the knowledge.

Contemplation of oneness gives you a deeper understanding of yourself. When you merge with oneness, suddenly you realize that you are boundless. From this perspective, personal achievement becomes an ongoing choice. The rapport you cultivate with the goddess and her consort empowers you in every aspect of your life.

When you engage in the merging process, mind generally moves through four veils or levels. The primary level of mind is one of vivid images. Images shift and float and even seem meaningless. Wondrous creatures from folklore, myth, and legend move with the merging mind. The countryside and buildings appear richly detailed and brightly colored. Your senses are heightened and light seems more luminescent. Scents are stronger. Music is more moving and textures are clearly defined.

31

The next mind shift while merging is usually at a personal recollective stage, sometimes considered to be the edge between the conscious and unconscious aspects of your mind. You may feel as though you are plummeting into the void and are reborn again, releasing the negativity of your past. Repressed emotions arise, and you can take this opportunity to relive and correct events.

From the personal recollective stage of mind, a deeper merge allows you to shift to the next level, a higher symbolic state. Here, you experience and act out symbolic initiations and explore personal myths using historical and archetypal forms. Often there is a flow and sense of the continuity of things. The facets of your life are depicted by mythical heroines and heros, goddesses and gods.

When you merge successfully, you know you are oneness. More light, more energy, and more joy exists in your life. Place your order at this restaurant of divine delights, where self-transformation and mystical union top the menu. Side orders of ecstasy and bliss are served daily. Permanent changes occur in your life when you dine at this establishment, when your individual consciousness blends and merges completely with oneness.

Gwyddonic tradition teaches three deep merges that lead to godhood. To begin, you merge deeply with the manifested universe to where you cannot perceive ego within yourself. Then, you merge deeply with the unmanifested universe to a place where there is no self. Finally, you merge deeply with both the manifested and unmanifested, discovering that they are one without distortion.

Those who desire to know more about merging may want to contemplate the following poem from the Elder Edda. It contains all the information you need in order to reach godhood and become the boundless.

The Lay of the High One

For all of nine stormy nights
I hung upon the tree,
Wounded by my own blade
Odin consecrated to Odin
An offering of myself to myself.
Bound to that mighty tree
Whose roots men know not!
None gave me to eat
None gave me to drink
Down into the abyss I wandered
And sought out the runes!
Then I fell into the darkness with a great cry!
Rebirth I attained
And also wisdom
For I grew strong and exalted in my growing.
Thus from one rune was I led to a second
From one act to another.

Merging techniques, paired with the contemplation of oneness and the knowledge that you are the boundless, can lead you to new levels of awareness while strengthening your abilities and offering you new vistas of self-discovery. Personal development in oneness affects all aspects of your life. Everything you come in contact with and turn your mind to seems to change in subtle, magical ways. Every atom, every cell, and every thought you have is altered after experiencing a deep merge with the boundless.

You rediscover that you are the light and the darkness. You become all sound and absolute silence. Each facet of your being seems infinite, and you are the continual, never-ending cycle. You constantly change yet forever remain the same. You are every mind and the vibrant energy of all nature. You whisper your name upon the

33

winds and see your face in every raindrop. You are the door, yet there is no door—only oneness and complete boundlessness.

The inner workings of the mind are more obvious and more easily comprehended as you merge deeper with the boundless. Personal awareness grows as you start to fully understand the manner in which mind moves and flows. Turning your mind to oneness at every opportunity increases your level of satisfaction along your journey with the goddess and her consort. The deeper and clearer you merge with the All Mother and All Father, the stronger your rapport with the many female and male aspects of the goddess and her consort. Incorporate these qualities within your being.

One way to enhance your merging experience is by using a portal of light. Portals of light are vortexes in time and space that defy the usual parameters of cause and effect. Well-constructed portals contain both the manifested and the unmanifested. They are mechanisms you create and utilize to generate high forms of energy. This energy can be moved, patterned, and made tangible, or unpatterned and dissolved at will.

Portals can be stationary or mobile. You may want to create a permanent portal for High Magic in a secret location. Every time you enter this permanent portal, draw a clockwise circle of white light around the area. To reinforce the energy of the portal, use clear crystal points on the four corners, starting at the North point and continuing sunwise to the West point. Keep in mind that these crystals represent the four elements of earth, air, fire, and water.

Mass amounts of pure energy are available in portals, creating a fertile ground for magical works. When you enter a portal of light, you exist synchronistically—in the primary being and in the double (a duplicate self that arises out of one's primary self). Hence you are able to move energy in an infinite array of patterns. The primary must exist in the manifested for the double to emerge from the unmanifested. The greater your experience becomes in the primary, the greater the potential in the double.

To move into the double, merge deeply and then project yourself outward. Your secondary self will begin to arise. This secondary self can take on any form. If you merge deeply enough, this form actually exists dimensionally in energetic reality. Use the double with wisdom and discretion. Afterward, the double returns to the unmanifested.

When you enter a portal, every atom in your body changes. This change is permanent. You shift your energy, mind, and perception. The objective then is to use this new information to update your views and add to your knowledge, leading you to new worlds and experiences.

Other worlds or realities are merely a slight alteration of perception or view. These other worlds co-exist in primary reality at all times, and are quantum-like. The question becomes one of how you perceive your world. Views are a collection of mirrors of the mind. Just as time extends beyond the past, present, and future, and relationships extend beyond birth, life, and death, so does reality exist beyond here, there, and elsewhere.

As you frequently experience these other worlds, primary reality becomes like an other world. Join us now as we take a brief detour on Bridget's Fire, through a portal of light to a magical land on a truly pleasurable adventure.

Guided Journey: Bridget's Fire

Wizards make love their own way. This tells the story of two such wizards in the Kingdom of Anu, on a small island called Belit....

She sits quietly on the golden upholstered chair, looking out the window. The morning sun shines, and she notices how it licks the dew on the leaves of the madrone and oak trees, turning the moisture into beautiful jewels gleaming within the branches. Her mind remains calm and expansive. Focusing on one bright diamond leaf, she moves her mind to another place, a small island she often visits called Belit, in the Kingdom of Anu. The island grows lush with vegetation and the soil smells rich and fertile.

She is known and welcome in this place. Her memories and experiences of Belit seem oddly more real than her normal waking reality. Perhaps they are. Mind makes an interesting tool of perception.

The Kingdom of Anu includes several island nations surrounded by pure warm azure seas. The nations share one technology based on crystals, and one science—the science of the mind. In Belit, the scientists act as wizards. She is a young wizard in training. Her teacher Achren is a wise woman with the title of Eldest Mother.

Achren is a great teacher, both young and ancient, and has a special fondness for the young woman. The teacher sees images of herself as a young girl in her student.

In a movement of mind and light, the young woman finds herself in the City of the Sun, at the bottom of the great stone steps that lead to the round tower room where her teacher waits. The vegetation grows thick here, the broad-leafed trees twisting and weaving themselves along the expanse of the stone steps, and up the roof of the tower. The young woman pauses for a moment to look at the patterns the trees create. She remembers the way her teacher always reminds her to look to nature for the answers; the plants, animals, fish, insects, earth, sky, and stars are wise beyond mere mortal imagination. Look for the things in common, and look for the differences.

Her loose white tunic and skirt glisten in the morning sun, blending into the bleached steps. Her hair shines like gold, pulled back in a long braid, tethered with a soft leather cord. Her body flows like a river, sensuously, as she glides up the steps.

As she reaches the top of the steps, she looks out over the City of the Sun. Free-form domes of various sizes and shapes hook together to serve as homes for the wizards. She smiles as she realizes that the wizards are the architects in this world. Their minds hold the structure of the Kingdom of Anu together with mental energy. The natural boundaries of the islands shift shape depending upon the communal state of mind of the wizards. Hence clarity of mind and intention are qualities praised above all others by the wizards of the Island of Belit. The young woman is blessed with powerful intention and is rapidly learning to control her mind with the help of her wise teacher.

She moves forward to open the heavy wooden door, hewn from the trunk of a huge tree. In the middle of the door, three interlinking spirals are carved in the weathered wood. She glides her hand over the carving, tracing the curved markings as the door swings open.

Her teacher sits elegantly on a stone bench in front of a large window. She smiles and looks directly into the eyes of the young woman, greeting her silently with her mind. In Belit they have a different way of speaking, a more precise way of communicating.

The woman in white takes her usual position at the left of Achren and waits for instruction.

Her teacher speaks silently, her thoughts deep and strong, "Remember to control what your mind moves toward. There is great power in this one concept. Flexible control is a wiser choice than rigid control."

She continues, "Always keep in mind the four basic concepts of instruction: love, wisdom, self-honesty, and self-responsibility. These thoughts should be ever present in your mind. Power and freedom ride under the cloak of these four primary concepts."

Her teacher's words have an odd depth to them, a deeper meaning. The young woman senses an excitement and intensity in Achren that surprises her, a portent energy. She smiles at her teacher, and reaches out and touches her briefly on her arm. The wise woman glows like an emerald. Her long silken robes flow over her body and down upon the wooden floor. She stands and raises her arms above her. Rainbows of light emanate from her hands and form an intricate lattice pattern.

"Work the pattern. The more you practice, the stronger your mind will become. Trace the pattern forward and backward, as you would in a game of chess. And remember what I have taught you. Certain points in the pattern are more crucial and have a greater effect on the totality. We call these cornerstones. Watch carefully for them."

The young woman merges with the rainbow lattice of light, flowing in and out of its brilliance, absorbing its energy and knowledge. Her mind grows and expands as she integrates her teacher's thoughts, more acutely aware now of the odd excitement and intensity in the wise woman.

Achren sits back down. She looks regal and splendid as the light from her hands swirls around her robe and through her hair, adorning it with shimmering stars of diamond light. She takes a large pointed crystal from the small table next to her. In an instant, the stone splits apart in two perfect halves.

"We are one, yet we are detached and distinct. Woman and man are one, yet they are different, two halves."

In the next moment, Achren weaves the stone whole again. "See the flow—oneness gives way to uniqueness which gives way to oneness. Woman and man are the same. In love, you will find this to be true. You will understand the deeper meaning very soon," she conveys, with a mysterious twinkle in her eye.

Just as Achren completes her thought, the young woman sees the image of a handsome, muscular young man. She feels his mind touch her intimately, and she responds fully in kind.

"He is your consort, your mate. You have chosen him with your mind. He will be here in a short while." Her teacher continues, "I assure you, your adventure with him will be extremely pleasurable. Allow yourself to merge completely with your companion. Gather together all of the tools I have given you and use them: mind, spirit, rapport, intention, and breath. Use your strength to be gentle. Remember the simplest way to enjoy the experience is to match, and then surrender to, the male energy."

Achren abruptly stands up, turns to the young woman and pulls her to her feet with amazing vigor, using only the light from her mind, emanating royal blue out of her palms. She cloaks the young woman in the deep blue light, shifting it to green, white, and then gold. The teacher's mind illuminates the mind of her student. It feels as though a veil lifts from the young woman dressed in white, a veil of fear and anxious anticipation. The wise woman calls out to the universe with her mind, "Blessed the bride the sun shines upon."

At the same moment, the door opens. The consort enters slowly, and moves toward the young woman with his mind and body. She waits for him and smiles.

Achren greets the young man with a caress of her mind, then moves to a small door in the back of the tower room, leading to a secluded and private garden. She opens the door and gestures with her eyes to her student and the man. Gently, she nudges them through the threshold and down into the garden.

"You have the place to yourselves. No one will disturb you."

The young woman and her consort flow down the stone steps, arm in arm. The thick branches of the trees in the garden weave a canopy above the lovers. Three birds sit together on a lower branch and sweetly sing. At the bottom of the steps is a silver basket filled with sweet cakes. Next to the basket on the flat rock are two glasses filled with clear liquid.

She picks up one glass, and he the other. Clinking them together softly, they toast the gods before drinking the honey-flavored liquid. Taking a cake from the basket, she breaks it in two and hands her consort one of the pieces. She eats the other. The ginger cake tastes sweet and spicy. They set down the glasses and move into the depths of the garden.

She smells the faint dampness of the ground as a velvety breeze strokes her face. The young woman and her consort embrace, breathing each other in. She smells of wildflowers, and he of morning dew and amber.

The garden grows around the lovers, with colorful flowers, exotic vines, lush grass, and majestic trees. In the center is a large pool of clear steaming water. A carved stone fountain, resembling a winged eagle, feeds it from a hot spring on its farthest bank. A sundial inlaid into blue and green tile leads up to the pool. The morning sun shines on it; reflections of time, stages of the cycle.

41

Hand in hand, the lovers walk toward the pool and sit on the grassy bank. The young woman dips her hand sensuously through the warm water and touches the man's lips with her wet fingers, before sliding her hand to the back of his neck and stroking his golden curls. She looks into his sky blue eyes, and as the gentle breeze strokes her hair and face, she leans toward him and kisses him on the mouth, tasting the wetness on his lips. The lovers move apart slightly. Close by, a golden bow-shaped harp lies against the trunk of an ancient tree. The young man moves his mind toward the instrument, and it flies into his hands. His fingers sound the strings of the sacred telyn, and using the jeweled tuning key, bring harmony to the twenty-one strings. He begins to sing to the lady beside him. His song tells the story of a young woman and her consort, and of the love they share.

She begins to hum the tune and then whistling along, enchants the garden to dance with her mind; flowers swing, rocks skip, trees sway, and small waves rise to and fro in the heated pool. He stops playing and sets the harp against the tree where the moving wind sounds it in a strangely relaxing melody. He sits back down beside his lover and slides closer to her, touching her with the side of his leg, his thigh, and finally hugging her in his strong and muscular arms.

The young woman responds and eagerly pulls off his unbelted tunic with her mind and she strokes his hard chest, starting at his shoulders, moving downward. His muscles tighten at her touch. The man's breathing quickens as he undresses her with his mind. Her body is lush; her breasts ample and firm. Her hips and thighs move sinuously around her lover. She embodies the perfect blend of flowing rivers and thrusting mountains.

He cradles her in his arms, and then carries her to the heated pool, where he slowly steps in, allowing the water to flow gently over their naked bodies. The water is soft and sensuous as it courses over their skin. They swim to the fountain in the silky water. A small waterfall spills from the eagle's beak, and the rushing water exhilarates the lovers as they move under the flow.

Sitting loosely in the eagle's talons are two brilliant stones, one emerald-hued and the other ruby-colored. The young woman holds the green stone while her consort holds the clear red stone. The round jewels ignite in a splendid array of color as the touch of the lovers' hands kindle the flame at the center of the stones. The sacred fire flares out from their hands and blazes into the universe. The young man returns his stone to the grip of the eagle's talon, and she does the same. They swim back to the opposite bank and climb out of the pool, sunning themselves on the grassy bank. Steam rises from their skin and dissipates with the light breeze. Her consort rubs his hands over her body, hovering over her like a great-winged bird. He strokes her velvety cheek with his hand. Her breathing intensifies, as her body arches to the tempo of an ancient rhythm.

He moves inside of her. She is moist, hot, and soft. Her consort is hard, pulsing, and eager. As he enters her, his mind whispers to her, "You are every lover. You are all love. I love you."

She feels as though she is being loved for the first time, as the bride of the sun. Her body quickens as he slides in and out of her. He moves quickly under her. She becomes pure flashing light and illuminates the garden with her mind while she mounts her consort and he thrusts up into her.

Sitting up slowly, he gathers her to him and carefully stands up. She feels him grow larger and more demanding inside of her body as he carries her around the pool sunwise three times. Their minds cry out as one mind, different, yet one.

They move beyond the garden into a portal of white light, and into the double. Their climax births the double, and speeds them to another dimension. A blinding white light passes between the lovers and shoots off into the sky. The young woman sees the very fabric of life, of light, expand before her. Time waits upon every sensation. She merges with him completely, deeply. She surges upward toward pure light, warm and inviting, and flies her lover to that light. Folding space, she lifts him like a great white owl lifts its prey.

He matches her, and sets his own pace. The consort encases her in a golden lattice of light, each movement more pleasurable than the previous. The woman spins her lover's lattice like a golden thread upon a spindle, rhythmically with care.

He takes the thread of light from her hand and encircles her in a ring of radiant energy. He moves the light completely around her and outward, his body hard, wanting more and more of her as he surges further inside of his lover.

She burns bright, hot with desire, full of herself, filled by her lover, humming like a crystal set inside of a grid of passion and flame. The lovers explode into pure light, merging to the deepest meaning as they become one.

We came from light. We are light. We return to light.

CHAPTER THREE

The Lady's Day
Hertha's Day

Viviana & Myrddin

And I wait for the Forest Spirit
The male deva, he is my mate
He is the one for whom I wait.

❧ The Lady's Day ❧
Hertha's Day

Viviana & Myrddin

The element is air

The Goddess and Her Consort

The spring equinox welcomes the Lady's Day, also called Hertha's Day. In Gwyddonic tradition, Tarvos is born on this Great Day. Hertha symbolizes the earth and acts as mother to Tarvos. The word "earth" is derived from her name. Hertha gives birth to Tarvos, who depicts a young aspect of Kernunnos. He portrays the golden one, and represents the birth of the sun which takes place near Coventina's well, the symbolic womb of the earth mother.

Traditionally, seeds are planted on the eve of Lady's Day as a tribute to the goddess and her divine gift to the world. The fertile earth goddess and her son are honored. All nature breaks forth in joy. The birds sing their sweetest songs and the animals, small and large, gather around to watch the birth of the golden one, the sun. As the days grow lighter, the goddess and her consort awaken and herald the beginning of spring.

The life mother Viviana embodies the aspects of birth and life. She symbolizes motherhood and childbirth, as well as children and love. She typifies the bright aspect of the All Mother and parallels the earth and water goddess Nimue, the Lady of the Lake. Nimue is a lover and student of the consort, Myrddin, who is more popularly known as Merlin the Magician. She acts as maker and keeper of King Arthur's sword, Excalibur.

The beautiful lady Viviana appears with sun-fire streaks in her hair, and has green or blue-green eyes. She is fair skinned with large, man-like hands. Her body reflects the goddess, and feels full and sensual, strong and supple. She nurtures the world, and has a delightful aura about her that makes all those who know her want to love her. She has an expansive and open mind. She moves light and quick like the wind, or fluid and full like the water of a lake. She comes to you in the forests, by lakes, by rivers, or on hillsides. In dreams, she represents the white lady of the oak, holding the eternal flame of knowledge.

The goddess Viviana holds the five-petaled rose while Nimue, her youthful face, is identified with swans, swallows, quartz and crystalline formations, along with underwater caves. Viviana exudes spring-like energy, vibrant green light, and she dresses in different hues of green, lavender, or golden-whites. Sometimes, she appears nude.

Viviana's consort is the sun and earth god, Myrddin. As a sky-god, he often lives in the woodlands with nature, and has a fondness for stones, caves, crystals, and herbs. Myrddin, a god of laugher and mirth, typifies the wild man of the woods and offers the world his gifts of healing and prophecy. He acts as bard and sorcerer, and is often associated with faeries or little people.

The consort Myrddin learned his magic from the goddesses Viviana, Nimue, and Morrigan. He is an expert shape-shifter, and he is often found in the forest near pure water springs and natural mineral deposits or in his crystal cave. He looks radiant and earthy, with woodland flowers tangled in his unruly thick hair, beard, and mustache. Most of the time, he appears with reddish tones in his hair and hazel green eyes. His symbols are the wild rose, sweet water springs, and a pan pipe that when heard gives the urge to dance and laugh joyously.

Myrddin resides in quiet, secluded places in nature, especially in heavily wooded areas with creeks or cool running streams. The consort smells of grass, leaves, the earth, and sweat. His face is rough to the touch, and he dresses in skins or goes nude. The sun earth god looks suntanned, and his chest is thick and muscular. He feels like the animals of the forest; the stag, the mountain lion, and the wolf. He stands like a great oak, a giant redwood, or a mighty pine. He flows from rivers, streams, and small brooks. If you listen carefully when you are walking in the woods, Myrddin will speak to you and answer your questions, sometimes in the form of a riddle.

Practical Knowledge and Useful Information— The Study of Nature

49

Goddess tradition follows nature. The story of Esus and Tarvos Trigaranus from the Great Book illustrates the continual cycle of the goddess and her consort, as they dance through the seasons.

> Long ago when the world was young, a marvelous and wonderful thing happened. In the early spring, near the pool of the goddess Coventina, a bull calf was born into the world. At a glance you could see that he was not an ordinary bull calf. His coat shone golden-red and his form was perfect. His eyes were the eyes of the sun.
>
> The golden bull was running about and playing, when out of the air descended three stately cranes.

They danced around him in a sunwise circle and he suddenly, very solemnly, bowed his head to them three times.

As spring wore on into early summer, he grew exceedingly fast and soon he was fully grown. Never was there a bull like him, and his fame spread far and wide. Animals, women, children, men, and gods came to look upon his great beauty. But wonder of wonders, wherever he went, the three cranes also went. They were his constant companions.

His days were filled with endless enjoyment, and the world was full of flowers. For in that ancient time, the world had never known winter.

Now Esus, the Hunter God, had been roaming through the fields and forests of the world looking for an animal worthy of his appetite, but he found no animal to his satisfaction.

Early one beautiful morning, he happened upon the meadow where he saw the bull and three cranes. One glance at the bull, and Esus knew that his search had ended. He drew his mighty blade and came upon the sleeping bull, but the cranes saw the danger and gave out a cry of alarm!

The bull rose to do battle with Esus. His golden horns were formidable weapons. The god and the divine bull clashed in combat.

They fought all day and all night, but neither could seem to best the other. The contest continued in this way for many days. It was on a night in the dark of the moon when the bull at last began to fail in strength. There under a great oak, Esus struck the divine bull a final deadly blow.

His blood poured out upon the roots of the oak tree and its leaves turned golden-red at that very instant for pure sorrow and grief.

The cranes made a great crying sound. One of them flew forward and in a small bowl, caught some of the bull's blood. The three cranes departed, flying toward the South.

An ominous gloom descended upon the earth. The flowers wilted and the trees dropped their leaves. The sun withdrew his warmth. The world grew cold, and snow fell for the first time. All humankind prayed to the All Mother to bring back the warmth, or all would perish. She heard and took pity upon nature.

The three cranes came flying back from the South, with one still holding the bowl. It flew to the oak tree where the divine bull had been slain and poured the blood upon the earth. Suddenly, out of the dust sprang the bull calf, reborn from Mother Earth! All nature rejoiced. Grass and flowers sprang up. The leaves budded on the trees. Thus spring came again to the world.

But the Hunter God heard of the bull's rebirth and sought him out. This was the beginning of the cycle which even to this day persists. Esus ever overcomes the divine bull, but Mother Earth ever causes him to be reborn. Let us pray that the Great Mother will ever cause his rebirth, and may we also forever be reborn.

The goddess tradition teaches us to carefully observe the cycles and to focus our intention and energy toward the seasons, so that they continually recur. This attitude is crucial to the balance and to maintaining the ever-changing, never-ending patterns of the earth. By helping the goddess, we help ourselves. We are one.

The story of Esus and Tarvos Trigaranus tells of a time when the world had never known winter, before the birth of the golden bull calf, who represents the sun. This indicates there was a period in history when the seasons were always pleasant, with no division or change in weather.

The cycle begins with Tarvos' birth, when the sun first breaks forth on the earth. With his birth comes the light and its polar opposite, darkness. Esus symbolizes the dark one. He slays the sleeping sun and brings grief and the cold winter upon all nature. The three gray cranes who dance around the sun are an important part of this solar mythology, as they are the keepers of the life blood of the golden one, Tarvos. As such, the cranes signify longevity and renewal.

Symbol and tangible reality blend and correlate. The All Mother, the goddess, issues forth from that which has no name, the unmanifested. She evolves and grows, and within her womb gestates manifested reality and its multitude of forms. Earth was covered in clouds during this gestation period. This was a time when the environment was constant, where plants and animals were similar regardless of geographical location. The sun, moon, and stars were not visible through this cloud cover, so the goddess was considered to be all things, and her presence was perceived as earth, air, light, and water.

When the goddess gives birth to the sun, all nature rejoices as they behold the golden one. But with this shining light, the earth loses its cloud cover and womb-like protection. Without this shield, the land begins to freeze and most of nature dies in the harsh cold winter. The winter ends as the goddess intervenes, giving birth once again to the sun. And so the cycle continues.

We are all fingers of the hands of the goddess and her consort. Participation in magical rituals on the eight Great Days help to keep us aware of our responsibility in the cycle of rebirth and renewal. Ritual also gives a deeper awareness of the inner workings of nature, and ultimately of ourselves as part of the greater whole.

The goddess tradition teaches the individual to apprentice oneself to nature. In her, the student can see the beginning and end of all patterns. Nature teaches us that patterns consist of a beginning, center, and end. Creation is threefold—birth, life, and death—just as we people are comprised of body, mind, and spirit.

Nature displays her contrasts of light and dark, hot and cold, young and old. The uniqueness and commonality of oneness is on exhibit as nature teaches us the contrasts of infinite and finite, of manifested and unmanifested. She openly shows us the prey and the predator, the host body and the parasite. She gives us water and earth, the sun and moon, as above, so below.

The plants have their own special knowledge to share with us. The oak tree teaches a strong magic as it puts forth a bounty of acorns that feeds the animals and birds. They, in turn, spread the harvest on earth to found future generations. William Blake stated it simply: "Does the Eagle know what is in the pit? Or wilt thou go ask the Mole? Can Wisdom be put in a silver rod? Or Love in a golden bowl?" Be prepared to learn patterning from an ant hill and the spider's web. Learn the elements of flow from the rivers and streams. From the ocean, the wind, and the birds, you can hear the songs of the seasons. The melody is like a cadence that is ever-changing, yet always repeating. Read the following traditional verse, and observe the cycle and renewal within its prose.

53

Poem of the Seasons

Leader:

> *I shall go as a wren in spring*
> *With sorrow and sighing on silent wing,*
> *And I shall go in our Lady's name,*
> *Aye, till I come home again!*

Group:

> We shall follow as falcons gray,
> And hunt thee cruelly as our prey,
> But we shall go in our Master's name,
> Aye, to fetch thee home again!

Leader:

> Then I shall go as a mouse in May
> In fields by night, and cellars by day,
> And I shall go in our Lady's name,
> Aye, till I come home again!

Group:

> And we shall go as black tom cats,
> And chase thee through the corn and vats,
> But we shall go in our Master's name,
> Aye, to fetch thee home again!

Leader:

> Then I shall go as an autumn hare,
> With sorrow and sighing and mickle care,
> And I shall go in our Lady's name,
> Aye, till I come home again!

Group:

> But we shall follow as swift greyhounds,
> And dog thy tracks by leaps and bounds,
> And we shall go in our Master's name,
> Aye, to fetch thee home again!

Leader:

> Then I shall go as a winter trout,
> With sorrow and sighing and mickle doubt,
> And I shall go in our Lady's name,
> Aye, till I come home again!

Group:

> But we shall follow as otters swift,
> And snare thee fast ere thou canst shift,
> And we shall go in our Master's name,
> Aye, to fetch thee home again!

In the modern world, many people find themselves with little or no time to enjoy recreation outdoors in the forest, fields, or by the ocean. Because of this, we become more alienated and separated from the earth. In turn, we become more distant and apart from ourselves. We walk on concrete instead of dirt, grass, or sand. We move in metal steeds across great expanses of asphalt, rather than on the backs of horses. We work in artificial environments and breathe machine-recycled air.

We often forget that we are an intricate part of nature. In our hurried lives, it is easy to lose touch with our natural rhythms and cycles. This is glaringly obvious as humankind continues to exploit and unnecessarily destroy the earth's resources. Fortunately, as individuals, we have the ability to learn that there is indeed an ever-renewing cycle, and we are part of it. From nature's examples, we can better understand the order and nature of our own existence, and help the efforts of the goddess instead of hindering her.

Behold! See nature as she is. As you seek the secrets of magic and self-development, first look to nature for the answers. She speaks the truth.

Guided Journey: The Lady's Day, Hertha's Day

The morning stretches into the warm and inviting afternoon. The wind whispers through the trees then grows
louder as the massive branches of the giant redwoods
sway gracefully. The sound fades for a time and then
grows stronger, only to fade quietly again. In the deep
green forest, ocean waves of air roll off the hills, and the
majestic trees dance.

The sun's rays penetrate the trees here and there,
slowly drying the forest floor. The beams strike immense
granite boulders and the megaliths shimmer like jewels in
the lush and ancient wood. Ferns grow between the trees.

Morning glory and blackberry vines twist up ravines and down small streams. Wildflowers bloom everywhere, splashing color on the carpet of green grass. Birds sing to the morning, to the lady, and to the Forest Spirit. He is her mate, and the one for whom she waits.

She sits on the ground, damp with the earth's sweat. All she touches is moistened by the invisible dew. The wind sings through the trees and the forest fills her senses. The scent of the oil off the needles heating in the morning sun blends with the moist soil and the wildflowers nestled among the grasses. The animals, streams, and rocks add to the perfume. The scent grows stronger as the gentle wind dances across her cheek. She breathes the forest in, deeply and completely.

She feels completely safe in the womb of the woods. She walks into a small clearing. Soft with new grass and hidden from all but the Forest Spirit, the secluded meadow exudes a delicate fragrance in the heat of the sun. The giant redwoods encircle the meadow and stand as reminders of the strength and power of the forest.

As she sits upon the grass, an owl flies closely over her head, dropping a crystal mirror into her hands from above. The owl swiftly flies over to a branch of one of the massive redwoods and watches the woman silently.

She holds the mirror in her hands. It feels amazingly lightweight and cool to the touch. The frame is made of silver metal twisted into a beautiful weave that ends in a circle at the base of the handle. She turns the mirror over and notices the three connecting spirals decorating it. She flips it back over and looks at her reflection in the crystal glass as a warm breeze tickles her forehead. The sensation relaxes and soothes her. The woman stares into her own mirrored face and merges deeply into the visage, into oneness. Her mind expands beyond her imagination.

She allows pictures to float slowly across the looking glass. As she merges deeper, she feels her essence drift into the mirror. The wind grows stronger. The green grass moves in its wake and settles back gently.

She looks into the glass beyond her own mirrored face and sees three images. Her animal nature stares back at her. The human woman and the goddess also watch her from the crystal glass.

The visions seem familiar somehow, and empower the woman. In the glass, she sees flashes of her future, changes, enhancements, and a complete acceptance of herself. Gradually, she sees the face of her mate the Forest Spirit next to her in the mirror—woman and man, unique, yet one. The images blend together as the sunlight hits the surface of the glass. She carefully puts the mirror down at the base of the tree where the owl stands guard. The wind swirls and tugs at the mirror, and the owl swoops down and picks it up in its talons before flying off into the distance.

The man beside her carries a staff made of wood with a brown satchel tied to it. He sets the stave against the massive tree. The lovers face each other, drinking in the image of one another. Arm in arm, they move toward the center of the clearing and sit down on the soft new grass. The spot is peaceful and comfortable. He notices the flowers a short distance away, walks over, and picks a five-petaled wild rose. He glides back to the woman and hands her the rose.

She takes the wild blossom softly from the Forest Spirit and breathes in the heady scent. For a moment, she hears the tinkling voices of children in the distance.

The man takes several packages from his satchel—a bag of seeds and three small fruit trees which are labeled as green, red, and golden apple trees. The woman finds several small green cone-shaped seeds from under the redwood trees, and she adds them to the packages. The Forest Spirit uses the sharp end of his staff to dig holes in the earth. The soil seems to give way with ease under the pressure of the stave.

She carries the seeds and trees to their new positions in the clearing. Together the lovers plant the trees in the larger holes, and the small green seeds in the smaller holes. Afterward, they cover their work carefully. Then, the Forest Spirit calls to the winds and he scatters the bag of wildflower seeds in the gust. Her senses vibrate. Alive with the wind, the earth, the water and the sunlight, she breathes in and merges with the land like a beautiful earth lady. Like the goddess, she flows free with the wind and dances with the trees. She hears swallows singing close by, in a perfect serenade as they dart back and forth.

He smells the ground, the earthiness of it. He tastes the water in everything around him, even in the sweet moistness of the woman beside him. His body hardens and quickens when he thinks of the pleasure she is about to give him and the pleasure he will give her.

59

The sunlight shines strong and hot on his back. Under the trees, the sun's rays filter through the canopy, and cast intricate shadows and patterns on the ground.

He lays her carefully down upon the sun-drenched grass, moist and cool.

Neither of them move. Gazing at each other, they share the same sensation of a fleeting glimpse of the core of one another—a flicker of the flame. It seems as though they are beholding each other for the first time, the last time, all times.

She sees shafts of light coming from his smiling eyes. The shafts transform into streams of energy. Like the web of life, pulling her to him, the light bonds them in the sacred rite of the cycle, forever and a day. Caught in a spiral of flame that consumes them, she does not realize that her eyes blaze as brilliantly as his.

She reaches up and touches him softly on the arm. This simple movement carries with it a feeling beyond intensity, in a realm where few dare to visit or travel. The exchange, the energy, and the vibrancy lift them from one reality to the next. Each touch and breath sets them spinning into another sensation of lust and emotion.

He tenderly brushes his lips over her forehead, then kisses her eyelids, and finally her mouth. The scent of her skin and the softness of her tongue fuels his deep and ancient desire as his caress finds the hollow of her throat.

She rubs against his chest and hips, trying to get closer to him. Her breath comes in sighs and sweet moans. She moves against him, and his body boils.

His fingers find the clasp of the soft green robe on her right shoulder and deftly unfasten it, pulling the fabric slowly from her pliant body. The velvety texture awakens yet another sensation within her.

As he pulls the robe over and away from her body, he yanks a handful of the grass from the earth beneath them and tickles her seductively on her neck. He brushes the grass between her breasts, slowly down the inside of her quivering thigh, and over her calf, ending at her ankle.

She quickly undresses him. As her urgent fingers seek to strip him of his clothes, the fabric groans then rips.

Her lover's physical strength and beauty astonishes her. She traces the hard muscles of his naked chest and shoulders with her eager hands, lightly scratching the surface of his skin with her nails.

He groans and moves to capture the hard tip of one her breasts with his tongue and teeth. Nipping softly, he feels her shudder beneath him. Then slowly he tastes the other, teasing the bud into perfection. Gently kindling the fire, his mouth moves lower to her stomach, and lower yet, as he savors her.

She cries out as his fingers, then his lips, find her secret cave, the sensations transporting her to another realm where touch, emotion, and desire are the sole dwellers. Her body quivers under his skilled tongue and she tangles her fingers in his silky hair, damp with sweat, as she firmly pulls his head down.

He fills his mouth with her wet softness.

She surrenders herself completely to the fierce melting urgency his mouth stirs at the core of her.

She feels her hands burning against his naked flesh. She presses lower, caressing and kneading, igniting his hard desire. As her hands explore him, they feel like giant branches of a redwood tree. The earth is her foundation, her soil, her nurturer. She is the spring tree, all green, immense and all-knowing. Her branches stretch around the Forest Spirit.

She cradles his maleness as she feels herself move beyond the clearing, expanding more and more, into the universe. She moves into the boundless and into oneness. She is a mighty tree holding the earth in her arms. She holds her lover as if she were holding the flaming sun in the sky. She sees brilliant green light beam off of her hands and her fingers as she cups and caresses her mate. The clearing becomes alive with the same emerald light.

Her lips and tongue move down her lover's chest, swirling over each nipple, down farther. She teases him and then tastes him, covering him.

She becomes aware of the sound of the wind through the trees. There is a pattern to it, rhythmic, softly whispering. Then it becomes stronger, building up in velocity and power. And then the wind grows quiet, gently murmuring through the undulating branches.

Her mouth, tongue, and fingers move with the same rhythm as the wind, arousing her lover more and more. He groans his appreciation as she covers him again and again, moving with the wind, her tongue swirling faster and faster, slowly stroking his hardness like a moist feather.

She lays back on the grass and reaches out to him. He comes to her without hesitation, and plunges into her like an osprey swooping down on its prey. He feels sharp, sure, and powerful. He moves into the deepest part of her. Stronger and stronger, he flies her higher and higher.

As he dives into her and fills her, she feels the light around them glowing, hotter and brighter, green then gold. Knowing takes hold where sensation leaves off. She sees him as he truly is, like a god, as every lover and every man.

He looks at her, his eyes filled with love and light, in awe of her skill, her beauty, and her ability to love with complete abandon. The wind blows through the clearing, softly whispering. She moves slowly beneath him, winding her legs around his. The breeze builds stronger, and he moves into her with the same tempo. The wind blows harder and harder and gusts through the clearing as the man dives into her well, faster and faster. The air becomes still again and the Forest Spirit moves slowly and deliberately in circles inside of her.

The grass cushions her back and the sweat from their bodies nurtures it with a salty potion. Her lover grabs handfuls of the grass as he thrusts himself deeper and deeper, driving into her moistness, covering her with his slippery body. He grows hotter, calling her name.

The wind echoes his words. The breeze builds stronger and stronger, as if it is challenging the woman and man, wanting them to take their love over the edge. The forest invites them to a place where the trees create the wind, only to lick and stroke lovers into ecstasy.

His eyes silently speak to her, pulling her like the current of a powerful river. She cries out to the Forest Spirit, to the wind, in pure pleasure, seeking more. The gusty wind answers her and it blows stronger and stronger, louder and louder.

Light fills her, shooting from her lover and lifting them to the fiery center of oneness. There is no separation. There is only union and perfect love.

They lay together for a time until the sun becomes too hot for them to stay in the grassy clearing. The shade of the giant trees beckons the lovers. Scooping up their clothing, the man picks up the staff and empty satchel, and they walk slowly into the forest. The scent of the ground and trees carried on the breeze, meets them as they move into the cool shade.

He drapes his tunic across the trunk of a tree, fallen years ago, now overgrown with ferns and moss. He lays her over the trunk on her stomach, and glides his hands over her soft skin.

His fingers knead her body and he gently licks her like a bear licking honey. The silken texture of his tunic caresses her breasts. He rubs himself against the back of her thighs, pulsing at each touch. His hair tickles her skin as he reaches down and cradles her swelling fullness.

Undulating in her craving hunger, she implores the Forest Spirit to enter her.

He stalks her like a great beast of the woods and takes her from behind. His body is hard and demanding, and he satisfies the woman as he moves with her like the wind through the trees. His breathing quickens, and his heart hammers as the forest moves around the lovers, dancing in the air. Love courses through them like a whirlwind,

63

spinning and carrying them, and then crashing down and lifting them up again.

He gathers the woman in his arms and sets her on the ground. She leans against the nearest tree, her legs unsteady. The tree trunk is gnarled and split at the base. She spreads her robe over the crevice and sits down. The woman stretches her arms out over the rough skin of the giant jutting tree as her lover strokes her body with the lightness of a feather, and then rubbing her more firmly in rhythm to the wind.

She finds two rounded knots in the redwood's thick trunk. She holds these tightly as the Forest Spirit kisses her fully on the mouth and moves into her. The woman calls out to the wind, and to her lover in pure pleasure. She winds herself tightly around him.

She feels waves of passion flow through her like pure heat. As their bodies move as one, she can feel him grow larger and more demanding.

He has incredible control of his body. He waits for her, enticing her, and stretches her past all limitation. Each layer of sensation is an experience of pure energy and delight.

As she moves with him, she feels every cell in her body rush rhythmically, heightening every moment. A tremor surges through her legs and arms, and flows through her breasts, hardening her nipples into crystal.

His touch feels like liquid fire burning her into surrender. Every atom of her being is alive, singing, glowing, waiting, and wanting more.

He thrusts deeper and deeper, and moves to the peak of union at the same moment as she. Time stretches into eternity as the gods stand before them, and beckon the lovers to a higher plateau. The faces of the gods flow through the woman and man like the wind through the trees.

The wind answers the lovers as it builds up stronger and stronger. She moans in satisfaction as wave after wave of climaxing light moves through her.

The Forest Spirit howls into the distance as he finally gives into the ultimate sensation of surrender and release. Shuddering and clinging to her soft form stretched beneath him, his breath comes in short, urgent rasps.

She feels the hammering of his heart against her slick skin, echoing her own. She becomes one with the maleness of the forest.

They lay entwined for several minutes as their breathing quiets. Neither move. They hold each other and drift off into a peaceful Lady's Day sleep. When she awakes, the Forest Spirit is gone.

CHAPTER FOUR

❧ Beltane ❧
The Adventure of the Sun

Belisana & Tarvos

Merging the past into the present
Your candle-lit eyes dance toward me
Like the ancient ones breathing
Like the circle of stones standing.

❧ Beltane ❧
The Adventure of the Sun

Belisana & Tarvos

Element is halfway between air and fire

The Goddess and Her Consort

Prancing and dancing, out of the east he comes. Beltane, the fourth Great Day, symbolizes Tarvos as a young lusty bull on an adventure of the sun. This Great Day falls at the beginning of May when the length of days grows longer and the light becomes brighter. Bel means "bright like the sun," hence the name of the ritual day.

Traditionally, Beltane begins at moonrise on May Day Eve. The Beltane rites are intended to increase fertility of the home, the fields, and the herds. The Beltane bonfire is lit with the spark from flint or friction, and contact with the fire is symbolic of contact with the life-giving sun. Women, men, and children customarily dance the Celtic holy round, clockwise circling the sacred fire. On the Isle of Man, rowan branches or twigs are carried three times sunwise around the fire to protect the house and bring good luck. Cattle are driven through the flames to prevent disease and improve the herds.

May is considered the month of sexual freedom. Like the Roman Floralia and other indigenous springtime ceremonies, Beltane celebrates the fertility and creation of life and the greening of spring. The Maypole, fashioned from the sacred tree, represents the phallus of the lusty young bull, Tarvos. When we dance around the Maypole we are revering the female and male principles of generation. The Maypole winding intensifies these powers by combining the serpentine and the double circle around the sacred green bough. The May Queen and King represent the goddess and her consort as female and male qualities of productivity and fruitfulness. She is the Great Mother and he is the Horned God.

Following is a song that is sung on Beltane morning which incorporates the symbolism of the female and male aspects in nature:

> *We've been rambling all the night,*
> *and sometime of this day,*
> *and turning back again, we bring a garland gay.*
> *A garland gay we bring you here,*
> *and at your door we stand.*
> *It is a sprout well budded out,*
> *the work of our Lady's hand.*

Belisana, a goddess of healing and laughter, is a female counterpart to the male consort, Tarvos. Belisana is a young aspect of the sun goddess Bridget. She is also an aspect of Belisama, a river goddess traditionally depicted as the goddess of the Mersey River in Britain. Belisana appears as the gentle sunshine lady of the forests. As an earthier form of the sun goddess Bridget, Belisana portrays the sun maiden, and her name means "bright and shining one."

The goddess Belisana communes with nature, talks with the animals and plants, and nurtures the earth by watering, sowing, feeding, cultivating, and protecting the creatures. She wears long flowing transparent robes of sunrise colors and a white mantel. Her golden hair hangs long and her eyes are blue as the sky. In her hands, she holds the rising sun.

Her mate, Tarvos Trigaranus, portrays a young aspect of Kernunnos, the All Father. Tarvos represents a god of vegetation, symbolized by the golden bull. He is full of loving energy and life. His stature varies, but he always has a bull-shaped body with a large chest, muscular arms, and thick thighs. The consort feels sensuous, strong, and virile. He is perfectly formed, and he appears incredibly handsome and dashing, with a spirited sense of humor and wit.

Smiling brightly, Tarvos looks very like the month of May. His eyes are large, clear and unusual, and he frequently wears bold and brilliant colors of green, gold, red, and blue. His companions are three gray cranes. The rituals of the Great Days follow Tarvos through his life, from beginning to end, on his adventure.

Practical Knowledge and Useful Information— The Four Elements

As you move along the path of the sun, notice how the elements of earth, air, fire, and water follow along with you on your journey. Gwyddonic tradition uses these key elements in both rituals and throughout the teaching. Each element is represented on the altar by magical tools, which are consecrated by the goddess and her consort.

The elemental altar pattern, using traditional tools, has its foundations in concepts that are both practical and metaphysical. Remember, elaborate and ornate tools are not a prerequisite to doing ritual. You can even choose to symbolically visualize your altar and tools, rather than using tangible items. Carefully select your altar tools. During initiation, representatives of the goddess and her consort consecrate and transform these special items into magical tools.

Position your tools so that you can move and use them at will. They should be on a sturdy surface that is situated in the North point. Traditionally, a green or red cloth embroidered with symbols of the goddess covers the surface. Some practitioners prefer to set their altars in the East corner, and start their rituals at the East point. Experiment and decide for yourself which method you prefer. Unless otherwise stated, our reference point for ritual will be the traditional North point.

Keeping in mind that your altar tools symbolize the four elements, you then represent a fifth element. Facing the North point and looking at the altar, first place the symbols of the goddess and god on the left and right, respectively, toward the center back portion of the surface. The symbols can be anything you choose, two rocks, two statues, two plants or any combination therein. Let your imagination run free. Next place a green candle on the left side of the altar next to the goddess, and put a red candle on the right hand side, next to the god.

The goddess side of the altar holds the feminine nurturing elements of water and earth, symbolized by a chalice of water and a bowl of salt. The wand, preferably one you have made yourself, rests on the goddess side of the altar as well. The wine cup, a symbol of divine love, rests at the center of the altar.

The male side, or god side of the altar, holds the power elements. These are a white candle, the symbol of fire, and an incense burner, the symbol of the air element. The athame, dulled for safety, also sets on the male or hot side of the altar.

Always remember to view the altar in its entirety. Consider all the elements as distinct, yet part of the larger picture and oneness. In addition to elemental aspects, the altar table reflects the integration between manifest and unmanifest metaphysics. The athame points to the unmanifest, and the wand points to the energy of the manifest. In this way, the elements are identified with the path of the sun and the cycle of life.

The wand dawns at the West point, from the water of life, and from her womb gives birth to the unmanifested. The seed is fertilized and grows in her womb, until it is born anew, rising toward the sun and breathing in the air. Each breath brings a deeper understanding, wisdom, and awareness. The growing seed travels ever toward the sun and the athame, which represents the unmanifest. Finally, the seed transforms in a fiery death, and ultimately, is reborn. The pine tree, symbolizing rebirth, must pass its offspring (its seeds) through fire before they can sprout and grow.

Vegetation transforms into fruit and then seeds. In this form, they are carried through the air and by animals. Fresh air and water enables the seeds to again begin their transformation as they travel toward the sun. Just as the plants, you have the potential to transform many times over in your lifetime. Move past your imagination and rediscover the boundless using the proper intention and a deep enough merge. You are an essential part of the spiral dance. Allow yourself to stay in step, keeping the basic elements and their deepest meanings in perspective.

As you build your rapport with the four elements and begin working with the four Wards, you will notice that your perception and wise use of energy and power will increase proportionately. The deeper you merge with the four Wards, the elements and all of their aspects, the stronger your rapport and connection will be to the energies they represent. One valuable way to enhance your interaction with the four elements is to associate them with areas of your mind and body.

Continually remind yourself that you are the elements. Your flesh and bones are the earth. The earth is your flesh and bones. Your breath is the air. The air is your breath. Your eyes are the light. The light is your eyes. Your emotions are the water. The water is your emotions. The more you practice this mind pattern, the closer your rapport will be with the elements and the representative goddess and her consort.

The element earth connects to body salts, minerals, and bones. Earth reflects fixed form and stable structure and corresponds to the nerves and brain. Air correlates to the content of mind, the lungs, body gases, and to the ears and hearing. The fire element provides heat and energy in the body, the light of eyes, and bio-energy. Fire also corresponds to oxidation and consumption. The water element controls the blood, oils, water, and the fluidity of the body, encompassing the body's flow and tidal response.

After you have set up your altar, you can then call in the four great elementals. First draw a magical circle and purify the area with salt by moving to the North point. After purifying the North point, continue on to the East, South, and West points, in that order. When you are finished, knock soundly on the altar with your wand nine times in three sets of three, with a momentary pause between each triplet.

Set the four Wards in place by calling a group of four great elementals to stand guard at each of the four points of your magical circle. Several sets of elementals are thousands of years old. Some sets of four are brand new. Others wait to be created. The Wards will respond to you if you merge deeply with the intent of communicating and asking them to guard the circle. Depending upon your desire, you can create a permanent set of four Wards or simply call in an already existing set.

The procedure for calling the four Wards is easy and straightforward. The altar tools symbolizing the four elements are brought into the center of the circle. Starting at the North, take the bowl with salt or earth, and sprinkle a bit on the ground. Set the bowl down, and hold your athame in your right hand. Lifting up your arms, speak these words in a strong and respectful voice:

> *Oh, great and mighty one, ruler of the North March, come, I pray you. Protect the gate of the North Ward. Come, I summon you!*

Move to the East, to the air element, and take the incense burner in your hands. Move the burner back and forth across the East point. Set the incense back down and hold up your arms with your athame in your right hand again, summoning the Ward by saying:

> *Oh, great and mighty one, ruler of the East March, come, I pray you. Protect the gate of the East Ward. Come, I summon you!*

Slowly and deliberately move to the South, keeping in mind that you are now merging with the element fire, denoting the sun and pure light. Take the candle and wave it at the South point. After setting it back down carefully, hold your arms out with your athame in your right hand and say:

> *Oh great and mighty one, ruler of the South March, come, I pray you. Protect the gate of the South Ward. Come, I summon you!*

Keeping your energy level high and your mind deeply merged, move to the West, the element of water. Take the chalice filled with water and sprinkle a few drops of the water on the ground. Set the chalice down and while holding your athame in your right hand, and your arms upward, say:

> *Oh great and mighty one, ruler of the West March, come, I pray you. Protect the gate of the West Ward. Come, I summon you!*

Move to the center of the circle and chant the goddesses and gods names:

> *Kerridwen, Kerridwen, Kerridwen, Kernunnos, Kernunnos, Kernunnos, ayea, ayea, ayea!*

Build the power up as high as you possibly can and then release it toward the pattern of energy you select. Swaying or dancing can enhance the effect of the final power level. The four Wards are now standing guard.

Guided Journey: Beltane,
The Adventure of the Sun

Eyes closed, the woman inhales deeply, totally filling her body with breath and energy. Letting go, her body becomes limp and she completely releases all the tension in her muscles. She breathes more deeply and her tension flows out with each exhale. Deeper and deeper she sinks into tranquility. Her body breathes on its own, naturally relaxing, as she feels more and more serene and peacefully aware. Her mind diffuses like a cloud into oneness.

Shifting her body, she becomes more comfortable and at ease. Breathing and relaxing deeper and deeper, she begins to focus on a single point of white light in her mind's eye. This light glimmers close by on the near horizon. She watches the light become brighter and brighter, clearer and clearer, and feels herself beginning to move toward it. The brilliance is warm and inviting, comfortable and soothing. She moves closer to the light. She imagines herself merging into and becoming one with the light. She is the light. The light is her. She shines in the rays of oneness, full of energy and life. Her mind keeps diffusing like a cloud into oneness.

As she opens her mind's eye, she sees a natural stairway made of earth before her. She moves down the nine earthen steps to a sun-filled place in nature. This place basks in an unusually clear bright light, and everything around her glimmers like freshly-painted colors and the light after a rain storm. She relaxes further, noticing the reflections of the forest all around her. She hears the sound of birds playing in water nearby and senses the breeze stroking her cheek. Each sensation sends her into an even deeper experience of knowing, trusting, and remembering. She feels her mind expand, bringing her a heightened awareness of perfect love and perfect peace.

The sun smiles knowingly down at her from the sky. She feels the rays of sunshine like fingers caressing her skin. A warm glow begins at her solar plexus, expanding until it fills her entire body with tranquil energy, a knowing that she senses within the core of her being, a remembering that beckons her ever onward.

She moves through the trees until she stands before a small meadow covered with a blanket of green grass and dots of white where daisies blossom out of the fertile ground. She looks closer, and sees a young stag dancing carefree through the meadow. His antlers look like small nubs as he moves his head from side to side. On the edge of the meadow, a small doe watches the stag for a moment before joining him in the dance. Together, looking like the King and Queen of May, they dance circles around the sun. The lady watches as the two deer simultaneously touch the fire of Beltane.

Her hand reaches down to pick a strawberry from the bush by her feet. She places the fruit into her mouth, and her teeth sink into its flesh. The juicy sweet liquid bursts in her mouth. She closes her eyes for a moment, becoming the taste. Opening her eyes, she notices the strawberry bush gives way to a grapevine that weaves through the grass and up a nearby tree, like a thread sewing itself into the fabric of life.

At a place up the vine, she sees a small dark brown pod hanging. As she watches, the pod begins to break into two halves. Deep from within the brown fibers emerge two yellow and black wings. She sees that it is a swallow-tail butterfly breaking free of its cocoon. The giant wings shake the last of the brown pod aside before gently swaying up and down. The butterfly glides through the air, flying for the first time. For a moment she becomes the butterfly, and the butterfly becomes her. Her mind diffuses like a cloud into oneness.

As she journeys on, she comes to a place where one stream diverges into two, and then again into one. The two streams surround a small island where a large gnarled oak grows out from the center. A gray squirrel scurries up its massive trunk. Next to the oak stands her consort, anxiously awaiting her arrival.

A small green bird flies past her, soaring effortlessly through the air. The gentle breeze directs it to the island. Once perched upon the thick lower branch of the oak, the bird begins to sing a most beautiful song for the lady. The bird sings a song of knowing and a song of remembering. It sings a song of Beltane and the eternal creation of life, springing forth every May out of Coventina's Well.

She moves closer until she stands before her lover, staring into the pools of his eyes. Her fingers stroke his wavy sun-colored hair as the two of them embrace for a moment of forever. With his body pressed tightly against hers, he feels like a young bull, strong, full of energy and the vitality of life. She senses the fire that waits to be awakened within him. Dipping into the well of creation, life becomes forever renewed.

After drawing a circle of white light around the island with his athame, the High Priest thumps the base of the oak nine times with his wand. He then calls in the goddess and her consort to each of the four directions beginning with the North point, and continuing clockwise:

> *Ayea! Ayea! Kerridwen! Ayea! Ayea! Kernunnos!*
> *Ayea! Ayea! Ayea!*

The high priestess then grabs a handful of earth, and hands it to him. Turning to the North, he raises both the hand with the earth and the hand with the athame above his head:

> *Oh great and mighty one, ruler of the North*
> *March, come, I pray you! Come, I summon you!*

He continues again, clockwise from the East to the South point, and then finally the West point. They act as aspects of the God and Goddess, every male and every female unto each other—All Mother, All Father, embracing in the renewal of life. After the four Wards have been called in, she raises her arms to the sun and sky and begins the ritual of Beltane.

The woman speaks:

> *Behold! He cometh! Out of the east he comes! His*
> *face with glory shines upon the earth.*

She pauses to feel the wind and sun on her face.

Behold! He cometh! Our bright lord in joyful mood,
prancing, dancing, out of the east he comes!

She looks to the east at the morning sun shining brightly down. All around her, in the sun, the wind, the water, and the oak, she hears the echo:

Prancing, dancing, out of the east he comes!

She feels her lover's arm around her waist, his hand warm and vibrant upon her hip. Their bodies join as one, hand in hand, side by side.

All around her, she can hear the life of the bright spring day erupting into play. She continues:

The wind whispers, Kernunnos! Lord Kernunnos!
Kernunnos! The birds sing, Tarvos! Golden bull!
Tarvos! The animals call, Golden one! Kernunnos!
Golden one! And all say, Behold! He cometh. Out
of the east he comes, Prancing! Dancing!

Again she hears the forest murmur as the trees and rocks whisper with voices that echo all around her:

Prancing, dancing, out of the east he comes! Ayea!
He comes!

The breeze moves through the branches of the oak, causing the new budding leaves to begin to dance back and forth. The green bird sings, the insects buzz, and the flowers blossom—life flowing into life. She marvels at the renewal of creation in the rite of spring, in this adventure of the sun.

The woman resumes the ritual:

Our bright lord looks upon all with kindest love.
He knows no sorrow, nor wishes any. The three
gray cranes love our lord. They know all sorrow,
but they wish none, so they dance! So dance now,
while you may. The seasons turn. Now is the time
to joyfully play! Away! Away! Away!

She grabs her lover's hand, and they begin a dance clockwise around the oak. They dance until they run out of breath. Laughing, the two of them fall to the ground beneath the giant oak. She feels the firmness of her consort's muscles as her hand glides across the forest of his chest. Her fingers feel like the grape vine weaving their way through the branches. She feels his skin hot beneath her touch.

He feels the softness of his lady's skin, like the petals of a flower, the opening of a blossom. He is like a bee, vibrating, buzzing, dipping down into her sweet nectar. She looks into the pools of his eyes. She says softly, whispering in his ear:

May the joy of our golden lord be upon you!

She caresses his perfect body. She hears him calling her to dance, a dance of spring, a dance for the lady, a dance around the maypole. He whispers back:

And you also, lady.

Her robe falls back, exposing the beauty of her body. Like a butterfly emerging from a cocoon, he sees her as if it were for the first time. He grabs her closer to him, caressing every inch of her skin with his lips. Their naked bodies dance through the flames of the fire. The embers, like a burning desire, are only satiated by water from the sacred well.

The lovers make love within the circle beneath the oak. Prancing, dancing, out of the east they come!

Letha's Day
Midsummer

Rhiannon & Manannan

I call your name softly in the darkness
You come to me, spilling into me
Your unveiled essence lifts us higher
As we cry out, one voice in the night.

꧁ Letha's Day ꧂
Midsummer

Rhiannon & Manannan

The element is fire

The Goddess and Her Consort

When the sun rises on Midsummer's morning at Callanish, on the Isle of Lewis in the Outer Hebrides, the people believe that the "Shining One" walks along the ancient stone avenue. His arrival is heralded by the cuckoo's call, a bird of Tir-nan-Og, the Celtic paradise and Otherworld.

The summer solstice marks Midsummer, also called Letha's Day. The word "Letha" means "death," the slow death of the sun. This Great Day falls on the longest day of the cycle and begins the negative half of the year. From Yule to Letha, the days get longer and the nights grow shorter. Belenus, the male consort associated with the sun, rules the positive half year when the light of the sun is more powerful.

Lugh, the male consort identified with the moon, rules from Letha to Yule, when his light is more powerful. Gwyddonic tradition tells the story of Tarvos, the lord of light, meeting with a lady dressed in silver and gray. She is Rhiannon, Lady of Avalon. In a basket on her arm are twelve golden apples. These fruit are from the Other-world, the Land of Avalon. The goddess Rhiannon gives Tarvos an apple to eat. He eats the fruit and it is very sweet, but it seems to cause a coldness in his feet. With a smile, the lady gives him another apple and it tastes sweeter still, but it seems to numb his will. The goddess gives Tarvos one more apple which he eats, but the cold-ness is so great that he refuses her offer of a fourth piece of fruit. She tells him with a smile, "Nine months of each year, the world has nothing to fear, for you shall be here for all to see. But for three months, you shall stay with me in the Land of Avalon, among the dead."

Rhiannon moves with the swiftness of birds in flight, often on the back of a white mare through the meadows. Frequently associated with horses, she is called the Queen Mother, or the Queen Mare. Rhiannon is graceful and fair, and her body is full and sensuous. She exudes a soft strength and is considered a goddess of birds, of nature and its ever-renewing cycle.

When the Lady Rhiannon calls to you in the woods, birds land next to you. All of her feathered friends embody her essence, and her eyes shine through theirs. Her magical symbols are a white mare, apples, and three birds. Her reddish-brown hair is long and silky, and her eyes shine a bright golden-green. The goddess wears bril-liant robes of red, silver, and gray.

Purveyor of magic, Rhiannon's consort Manannan is the son of Llyr, the sea god. Like his father, the Britons and the Irish considered Manannan a god of the sea. He possesses a magic coracle, called the Wave Sweeper. He also rides a horse or drives a chariot across the ocean. His other possessions include a mantle and helmet of invisi-bility and a magic wand. Manannan carries a golden spear and a sword named Retaliator. He uses these magical tools for manifesting and shape-shifting. The glint of his sword is one way to recognize him.

The Land of Promise, an Elysian island, is home to the consort. Thought to be a good provider, Manannan settled the Tuatha De Danann in the faery mounds of Ireland and established feasting which protected them from old age. At the feast, pigs were killed, eaten, and then returned to life again. He gave Cormac a golden cup which broke in pieces when lies were told over it, but became restored when truths were spoken.

As a master shape-shifter, Manannan uses his shifting abilities as if they were cards in a deck. His animal forms include the dolphin, falcon, panther, and wolf. He moves quietly in the shadows, hidden from view. The consort is active and travels in time and space. He exhibits mastery in all things, and he represents infinite creativity.

After midnight, Manannan visits dressed in black. His eyes are so dark that you cannot see his pupils. His hair is dark and thick. He moves like a cat, slick and fluid, with great speed. Patience is one of his virtues, along with a passionate nature that edges on wildness. The consort smells like the night, damp and spicy, or like salty ocean waves. When he speaks to you, listen. He can teach you the shapes of things to come.

Practical Knowledge and Useful Information— Moons of the Cycle

The rituals of the High Moons, like the eight Great Days, center and attune you with the energies of the cycles and seasons. Since ancient times, the phases of the moon, caused by the changing angle at which its lighted surface is seen from the earth, have formed one of humankind's best methods of monitoring time. The fertility of the goddess depicted by the female menstrual cycle correlates to the twenty-eight-day-plus cycle of the moon. Planting cycles are based on moonlight. During the full moon, plant crops that grow above the ground, and during the dark of the moon, plant root crops.

The moon is silver and the sun is gold. These two heavenly bodies figure predominantly in folklore. Native American mythology calls the moon the night luminary and the sun the day luminary. In all cultures, the moon is honored. On the full moon, Jewish Passover is celebrated. Christians observe Easter on the first Sunday following the full moon after the vernal equinox. The Greek goddesses Artemis, Selene, and Hecate symbolize the moon.

The goddess of the moon rules over all water. On the coast of Wales and Brittany, tradition says that people are born when the tide comes in and they die when the tide goes out. The flowing tide represents life, exuberance, and prosperity, while the ebbing tide depicts death, weakness, and failure.

Lunar positioning and intensity influence feelings and emotions as well as instinct, imagination, and receptivity. Astrologers wisely use this concept for forecasting and patterning. The moon also represents sensitivity, sensation, fecundity, and maternity. Beginning on the first full moon after Yule, the moon cycle contains twelve or thirteen high moons each year. The first full moon is called the Wolf Moon. It is a time of unity and purity, symbolizing rebirth, and regeneration. It is associated with the goddesses Morrigan and Medb. The second full moon, or Storm Moon, represents the polarities of germination—as above, so below. The Storm Moon is identified with the goddesses Bridget and Epona.

The goddesses Arianrod and Triana are associated with the Chaste Moon, the third full moon after Yule. This moon's energy is that of the Trinity: the maiden, mother, and crone. Following the Chaste Moon is the fertile Seed Moon, honoring the goddesses Coventina and Hertha, and representing the four elements of manifestation. Moving toward the month of May, the Hare Moon teaches control of the self and our physical manifestation, with the help of the ladies Danu and Etain.

The Dyad Moon, symbolic of time and union, is the sixth High Moon after Yule. The goddess Mei is identified with the Dyad Moon. The next moon, the Mead Moon, honors the goddesses Rhiannon and Artio. This is a time of etheric harmony, lunar fertility, and lucid dreams.

On the Wort Moon, Viviana and Rosemerta offer protection and knowledge. This moon represents the yearly cycle and purification. The goddesses Fliodhas and Sadv welcome you on the Barley Moon, the ninth High Moon of the cycle. Magic, healing, and wisdom prevail on this night. Nantosuelta and Boann herald the vintage season and the Wine Moon, while offering the gift of prophecy on this bright night.

The Blood Moon is identified with maternity and fecundity, and the goddesses Morgana and Andraste. The twelfth moon, the Snow Moon, represents divine or royal purpose. The goddesses Sirona and Danu give gifts of music, healing, and magic on this magical night. Finally, on the thirteenth moon, the Oak Moon, Kerridwen, the All Mother, teaches us rebirth and transmigration.

Each year on the Dyad Moon, halfway on the path of the sun, you may ask the goddess to grant you a boon. The boon is a reward for your positive energies and good works of the past year. The Boon Moon is identified with the mastery of time. You will need to ask a fellow practitioner to assist by performing the part of the goddess. If you belong to a group, the High Priestess traditionally acts as goddess. Be careful in your asking, as the goddess may lay a woe on you if you have been careless and negative in your works over the previous year.

After the traditional moon ritual and any healings, the High Priestess or suitable representative of the goddess retreats to a separate room. The door is closed and only candles light the room. Incense burns, and a small magical circle is created by the High Priestess. She sits or stands inside the circle. The members outside gather together and draw lots to determine the order in which they will enter the goddess' room. Using a deck of Tarot cards is the best method. The person with the highest valued card enters the room first, with the lowest valued card holder entering last.

Having chosen the highest card, you are ready to ask for your boon. You knock firmly on the door, enter slowly, and then kneel before the goddess.

The goddess asks:

What is your name?

You give a false name:

I am owl.

The goddess asks again, this time a little louder:

What is your name?

You answer again with a false name:

I am dragon.

The goddess looks you straight in the eyes, merges with you and asks in a strong and powerful tone:

What is your name?

The third time she asks, you give your true magical name. The goddess then calls you by name and says:

I know you and know you full well, for I have seen your comings and goings.

She calls you by name once again and asks:

What do you seek?

You respond:

Great One, I pray that you will grant me a boon.

The goddess addresses you and says:

I have known you and I have seen your comings and goings. I have seen your good works and honest effort.

The goddess then mentions something that you have done in the past year of positive value, and adds with intensity:

I will grant you your boon! What is your will?

At this point, if you unfortunately receive a woe, the goddess tells you of your negative doings and says:

I will not grant your boon, but on you I lay this woe.

She calls you by your true name and then gives you a task to perform for the benefit of others. You respond by saying:

Though the woe lays heavy on me, I know it will be to my good.

Bowing three times to the goddess, you depart the room, at the same time saying:

Blessed be! Blessed be! Blessed be!

If you are granted your boon, you say to the goddess:

I pray Great One, that you will grant me this boon.

You then tell her what it is that you desire. Your imagination is your only limitation. A boon can be as tangible as a new house, or as nebulous as a state of mind, perception, or view. It is your personal choice. You should choose your boon wisely, preferably in a merged state, and always as ecologically as possible, so that the consequences of your boon will be positive to those around you. When you have asked for your boon, the goddess addresses you by name in a firm and commanding voice:

I grant it to you.

With exuberance you say:

Praise be to you. Blessed be! Blessed be! Blessed be!

Bowing three times, you then depart with gladness in your heart.

Solitary practitioners can use these instructions by energetically merging with the goddess and asking her for the boon. Remember, all of the aspects of the goddess and her consort are qualities within each one of us. The High Moons are yet another way to tap into the energetic spiraling energies that permeate the ethers, waiting to be patterned.

I invite you now to travel with the lovers as they explore the ancient standing stones on the eve of Letha's Day, on the night of a full moon.

Guided Journey: Letha's Day

The evening is dark but for the moon and stars. The air feels moist and full of summer. Crickets sound in the evening's song, and an owl hoots three times and stops. Occasionally dogs bark in the distance.

At the bottom of a low hill, our horses drink from the stream at midnight. In the stark light of the full moon, I can see three earth mounds in the valley below.

We start up the hill slowly, passing by a giant, upright stone, a natural symbol of male energy and manhood. The horses snort as they pass the menhir and move quickly up the incline to our destination.

At the top of the ridge, the ancient sacred site stretches before us. The skyline and valley lay behind us, the countryside aglow with moon fire.

As we come to the edge of the stone circle, we slow the horses to a standstill. In front of us loom two mighty dolmens with a large capstone hanging on top of them. Giants dined at this immense rock table. The placement of the capstone is high enough for a horse and rider to pass beneath. I lead the way as we move single file under its shadow and into the center of the ancient site. We dismount and drop the reins of our horses on the ground. The animals stay in one place, standing quietly. In front of us is a large rounded stone with a large hole in the center. The sun and the moon are carved roughly in the face of the rock. I crawl through the hole, and you follow, clasping my hand firmly. The passage through the gap creates a shifting of our minds, renewing our connection to the vitality of life and to all things whatsoever they may be. We move into oneness.

We stand closer to the sarsen boulders. Carved faces of laughing maidens, an old hag, a horse, and a stag stare at us in the moonlight from the stones.

I whisper the names of the goddess and the god to the mighty stones, to the moonlight, and to the stars. The immense dolmens sing back to me in a midnight serenade.

I touch the stone closest to me, and watch as a bluish glow pushes at my hand. The power of the light grows stronger and warm on my palm, before dimming as I move my hand off the stone.

You call my name softly in the night. You conceal yourself behind a large menhir and move toward me dressed in a deep indigo blue tunic and pants. You move quietly like a cat; I cannot hear your footsteps as you approach. You now wear a black mask. Only your eyes show through, eyes so dark that the pupils blend with their color.

I stand completely still as you dance in front of me, dancing a circular motion, moving sunwise and upward around the spiral path, renewing the earth's energies, and creating a vortex of light. Your movements flow like the air circulating around me. You play with me and my mind.

I gesture for you to remove your mask, but you refuse. You like the disguise and tease me with it.

I pull back into the shadows of the ogham-carved dolmen and you stop dancing and stand in front of me. Quietly you take off your mask and smile at me.

We are drawn together by our eyes, shining reflections in the moonlight.

You draw me to you, kissing me softly at first. Then you kiss me longer, and then again, even longer. I can feel the outline of your lips, the inviting wetness of your tongue, and the smooth coolness of your teeth. You taste sweet and salty. Your breathing grows rapid and strained.

95

My heart hammers and my legs melt. I lean against you, keenly aware that you are holding me upright.

You kiss me again, your hands moving across my forehead and through my hair. Down over my shoulder and forward, they continue to the tip of my breast. You pause there, softly fingering the point as you nibble my tongue with your teeth.

My body shakes and trembles with your every touch. Your fingers and hands are like liquid fire flowing into each pore of my skin, every inch of my being. Your touch is hot and alive like moon fire.

Some ancient being within me, within the earth, pulls at you energetically like a magnet. A sphere of gold light moves into you, into me, hot and glowing.

You kiss me again before we move apart and walk over to the horses. You untie the blanket off the back of your saddle, and I take a small bag off the horn of my saddle. Pulling out two apples from the bag, I take a bite of one, and give you the other. After you take a bite, we both give the remaining pieces to the horses.

We move to the center of the circle of stones. There is a long, flat, and smooth rock half-buried in the earth. Carved figures, spirals, cup, ring, and channel markings dress the front of the stone as though it were an entrance with the threshold long covered by weather and history.

You spread the blanket over the stone before lifting me up in your arms and carrying me to the ancient bed.

I look into your eyes and beyond, out over the valley to the lights twinkling in the distance. The air, still moist, seems damper. My skin tingles with the wetness of your touch which blends with the warm breeze coming off the hills from the south.

I whisper your ancient name and beckon you to come closer. You come to me hot and wanting. You nestle next to me, coming as close as you can without crushing me.

I feel a fire burning inside of you, and your skin feels hot to the touch.

You slowly slide your hand down the front of my blouse and unfasten the golden buttons, one at a time. You touch my skin underneath each button. Your hand feels like a torch each time you touch me.

With each button that comes undone, another part of my mind comes undone. Another part of me opens up to you, to something inside of both of us, drawing us nearer and nearer to that place—a place of souls and fire, where hot passions blaze, smoking and flashing. Only lovers know that place of intense light. A light that is the dwelling place of dragons and dreams at midnight.

Quickly pulling off my blouse, you begin to work at freeing me from the rest of my clothes. Each time you remove something, you touch and tickle the skin beneath. I feel you acknowledge each part of me, each cell, each thought and response, as we step in rhythm to an ancient dance. You seem to know the cadence as if by instinct and I dance along, eager, waiting, knowing and remembering.

My body hums as I sit naked next to you. I take a deep breath and move my hands to your throat. As I reach the opening of your collar, I feel the stiffness in it, and the stiffening in you as my hand softly brushes the skin at the base of your neck. My leg moves into and around your thigh and calf, rubbing against the fabric of your pants. I enjoy the sensations of your hands and lips as I savor my exploration. We continually rub up against one another, repositioning and touching another hidden part of my body, your body.

I undo and open your shirt, stroking your bare chest. My fingers glide along your hair, across your nipples, and then caress the outline of muscles on your stomach.

My hands travel lower and tug on the waistband of your pants. Without hesitation, you unfasten and slide them down, away from your body.

Our bodies glow beautiful in the moonlight, strong like the light, supple like the night.

Our breathing is fast and strong. You pause and take my face in your hands while looking me straight in the eyes for the longest time.

I see things that I see in dreams, in starlight. My mind moves beyond my imagination. I look with desire, with fire, with wanting.

You look with memory, promise, and the light of a thousand suns. The world stops for a while as my lips

97

move closer to yours, pulled by desire, by the shape of your mouth, and the softness of your tongue.

You bend your head down to my breast and taste the nipple with your mouth, savoring it, driving me wild with each movement.

Your hands reach down between my thighs. Your fingers are rough against my silky skin as you stroke and coax my legs apart. Your fingers move into every part of me.

I am wet with desire as the night is damp with dewy moisture. I moan and encourage you as you move your mouth to my stomach and down to my center, licking softly and nibbling gently.

I lay stretched on the long stone, my arms above my head. Runes are etched in the flat rock above my head and you are crouched between my legs.

You move your mouth over my breasts one at a time as you leave your fingers inside of me. You kiss me over and over again.

Soft noises come from my throat. I want to touch you, feel you in my hands and in my body, fire in water, steaming. You are hard and respond with even the slightest touch. You want me. I want you to wait a little longer.

I push you back, and you lay stretched next to me on the blanket. I trace spirals and circles over your skin in the bright moonlight. My fingers move up and down, then sideways from left to right, shaping a cross on your chest.

My hands feel as though they are moving across a great land. Across universes, they move to the harmony of the spheres. As goddess and consort, we blend with the massive earthen henge.

I use my tongue to circle you, licking and sucking, my warm breath blowing on you like the moist breeze coming off the distant hills.

You grip my head, tangling and gently pulling my hair through your fingers as you groan your appreciation and satisfaction.

I mount you slowly. You look me straight in the eyes all the while, seeing every nuance, every emotion, knowing and remembering. In the light of the fiery moon, your eyes are glowing, fibers of gold and white light moving through you into me, an ever-renewing exchange.

Mated together, we merge as one into the night. We are pure light, flowing and moving across oneness. We can travel anywhere we choose, create worlds and star systems, merge into infinite lifetimes, into oneness.

Our breath rages. You moan and murmur words of endearment as I ride on to the deepest meaning. Your hands grip either side of my hips and hold me over you. You slide your hardness out of me slowly, then pull me down on you, and drive into me.

I gasp and cry out, suddenly exploding inside, my muscles contracting in and out and moving me into the next sphere of light, so much more light. The fiery glow flares off our bodies and into the massive stones around us.

You drive farther and farther inside of me, faster and faster, holding me into you, directing the movements of my hips, kneading and fingering my breasts. You push into me, panting. You speak my name over and over. You whisper the name of the goddess. I ride on, seeing pictures, seeing thoughts, seeing everything framed in brilliant light. There is so much light. I am on fire, aflame, and flying through the universe like a runaway sun hurdling out of control.

I am breathing hard. I can taste the stones and earth as I chew the air. The sounds of our love-making reverberate in the immense circle of rock, echoing louder, ancient voices in the night.

The stone circle spins around us slowly and steadily. The motion creates a hot wind that pushes me on. Sweat trickles down between my breasts, and wetness flows out of me onto you as you move in and out of me, each thrust slippery and fulfilling.

I move my arms up and out, casting and catching light. I soar into you and out, running the brilliant moon fire into the stones, into the universe, forming thought, being, matter, and creating anew.

I drift in the arms of the goddess, carried on a journey upward by the god on his flaming arrow of love.

We are for a moment truly the goddess and god, the lady and her consort, the All Mother and All Father. Together we renew the vital forces, the life impulse. Woman and man as one, we spin the earthly cycle as we spin with the ancient stone circle, toward the sun, to the glowing moon.

The blanket is rough on my knees. The hardness of the rock holding us reminds me of your hard strength as the hot wind from the spinning circle drenches us in its fiery breath.

I ride on, spurring you higher and higher toward the moon, riding to the night's fire. We gaze at each other, gazing at the moon and the stars as they appear in the night sky. Soaring, diving into the light, we clasp like giant falcons mating in flight. You rise stronger and stronger inside of me, your words incomprehensible.

I swoop down deeper and deeper, and you thrust harder and harder up into me. Our bodies consume one another in a never-ending hunger. Your hands play over my breasts and thighs, imprinting them with sensation and intention.

We spin with the stones, sunwise, faster and faster. In the spiraling light, I reach out to you, stroking your neck with my fingers. You are every man and every lover.

Running the light, we transform into pure energy and merge deeper, all the way into oneness. Knowing we are the boundless, we rediscover the entrance to the well of the lady.

With each movement now, I am more aware of you, of your breathing, of your essence, your feeling, and your love. I see you anew.

Your voice rasps, and you call out to me, calling the goddess. Crying out in the light, you flow into me, spilling your essence and your soul into me.

My body contracts and releases, sending me into a space so profoundly beautiful that I laugh out loud.

Our voices laugh and dance as one voice in the night.

The stones stand silent once more. The moon is ablaze with delight as I whisper in your ear, "I love you."

 Lughnassad

Rosemerta & Lugh

My skin tingles in a soft melody
When I think of the sparkle in your eyes
Like sun upon cool water
Your laughter as it dances
On a westerly wind.

❧ Lughnassad ❧

Rosemerta & Lugh

The element is halfway between fire and water

The Goddess and Her Consort

Held at the beginning of August, Lughnassad commemorates the wedding feast of the lusty god Lugh and his beautiful lady, Rosemerta. "Nassad" means "to give in marriage." In Gwyddonic tradition, Lughnassad is the only Great Day ritual performed by the High Priest. He represents the god, whereas the High Priestess represents the goddess.

On the river Boyne, the great festival was held at Teltown, which was named for Lugh's foster mother, Taillte. She is said to have died upon a mound in the village. Lughnassad was held as a memorial to her death, and the symbolic death of the goddess. At a place nearby called the Hollow of the Fair, women and men were married in reverence to the union of the sun and earth. Interestingly, from Lughnassad to Beltane, along the path of the sun, is a period of nine months, a full gestation cycle.

The celebration of Lugh's wedding honors the ascendancy of the moon, and is held just after sunset on the eve of the Great Day. It marks the time when the forces of light and dark converge. Two portals exist at this time, one just before sunset and one just after. The manifest joins with the unmanifest, creating both death and rebirth. When the goddess joins with Belenus, she resonates the light of the sun and the vibrancy of life. When the goddess Rosemerta weds Lugh, who represents the brightness of the moon and the aspects of night, she marries death.

Ancient people viewed death in terms of rebirth, of energies moving from unmanifest to manifest, back to unmanifest. Nothing truly dies in this sense. Things merely transform into different types of energy. In keeping with this viewpoint, natural death makes possible the many wonderful gifts of fertility and abundance. The wedding of Lugh and Rosemerta parallels that of Pluto and Persephone. Pluto mastered the unmanifest and he gave great wealth to those who incorporated honesty into their lives. Lugh, like Pluto, gives great treasures. He possesses mastery over all the arts and crafts, and is accepted as the deliverer of the Tuatha De Danann, the children of Danu.

When the goddess marries death, embodied by Lugh, she joins with the wisdom of the unmanifest. The destruction of the Corn Mother symbolizes the death of the goddess. This ritual takes place on Lughnassad, Hellith's Day, or Samhain. Each of these Great Days represents some aspect of death. Like the phoenix arising out of the ashes, the goddess, too, springs forth. The autumnal death of the Corn Mother leads to a new birth and a new spring. The last corn sheaf, considered sacred, is drenched in water and held as an emblem of the goddess and abundance. The random selection of a lord and lady to reign at the feast is one of the Gwyddonic customs honoring the wedding of Lugh and Rosemerta. Crowned with flowers, they depict the goddess and her consort on this Great Day. The lord and lady grant each member the answer to one special question they may want to ask. This tradition has its foundation in the ancient belief that death, master of the unknown, certainly knows the answers to all questions.

The consort Lugh, besides symbolizing the moon, is a solar deity represented by the setting sun. He has mastery over carpentry, poetry, history, and sorcery. Lugh serves as a harp-playing bard, a smith, and lord of war. He trained under the shape-shifting god Manannan, who bestowed upon him his magic sword, armor, and horse. He carries a bag of coins denoting his generosity. The cock, goat, and turtle are associated with him.

Every goddess' and woman's heart melts at the sight of the handsome, supernatural horseman Lugh. He makes poetry magical and causes music to heal. He loves singing and melody. Lugh has an insatiable sexual appetite, and a deep appreciation for the goddess and all women. He loves and protects the ladies. As a favorite consort, Lugh represents skill, wisdom, and abundance. Known for giving gifts of land and inheritance, he is a master of manifesting from the unmanifest. He exudes a mysterious warmth, and he possesses a powerful sense of humor and a zest for creating new things.

Lugh's hands feel rough to the touch, as though he has been working with them a great deal. His face is clean shaven, and his eyes shine a brilliant sea-blue. The well-loved consort smells of sandalwood, the hills at sunset, and the sea. He wears the colors of the setting sun: red, orange, gold, peach, and crimson.

The tradition of handfasting on Lughnassad lives on, as many practitioners marry on this August Great Day. Lugh acts as consort to Rosemerta, the goddess of love and abundance. Her name means "rose mother." The lady Rosemerta's beauty stems from the beauty that creates all beauty in the world. She typifies the true love that every man desires and longs for, and she, like Lugh, is associated with material wealth and prosperity. The cornucopia flowing with an ever-renewing supply of food and treasure serves as her magical symbol.

Lugh calls Rosemerta his Little Flower. She portrays a mother aspect of the Welsh goddess Blodenwedd, who was created for Lugh by the magician gods, Math and Gwydion, out of flowers of the oak, broom, and meadowsweet. Rosemerta is sensual and soft like the petals of a flower, and her kisses are moist like the morning dew. The goddess seems ageless. She has long hair the color of honey, and warm brown or greenish-brown eyes. Rosemerta smells like flowers, and wears robes the colors of roses: red, white, yellow, peach, and pink.

The intense desire between the goddess Rosemerta and her consort Lugh depicts the union possible between women and men. Rosemerta is truly a sensuous lady, and Lugh is a lusty god. That much is certain. She could use some helpful assistance with her all-consuming consort.

Perhaps a pooka or elemental would be a useful companion to our lady. You may ask, "What is a pooka?" You are invited to read on and discover new realities. Go ahead, climb into the looking glass, and let your imagination roam free.

Practical Knowledge and Useful Information— Making Elementals and Pookas

You can create elementals and pookas for a variety of uses, both for yourself and for others. In Gwyddonic tradition, these creatures are usually pleasant and helpful, and bring joy to their originators. These simple instructions give you the basics for making effective elementals and pookas.

An elemental is generally used for a specific task, whereas a pooka does many tasks and acts as a personal companion. A pooka is customarily worn or carried on your person, but this is not necessarily true of an elemental. The guidelines for making a pooka parallel those for making an elemental. The only difference between the two techniques lies in your expectation and intention.

Practice the following directions several times to hone your skills in making pookas and elementals. Once you have mastered these methods, feel free to change the guidelines to suit your personal style. Like any other work of magic, the key factors for creating these energetic beings are the Three Eyes of Kerridwen: expectation, desire, and merging.

Know specifically what you intend to create before you begin. Understand every detail of your program or formula. An error in calculation will result in an error in situation. Be sure you know what qualities you expect in your new elemental or pooka, and that you truly want them with every fiber of your being. Your success rate pivots on the strength and clarity of your expectation. You are the creator, and your creation will reflect your attributes and abilities.

109

First, determine the nature of your elemental or pooka. Carefully consider all of the parameters involved. Take sufficient time to picture your new energetic being. How long will the elemental or pooka live? The choice between a life span of a few moments or a few thousand years gives the creature its temporal character. It may perform only one task and then return to the unmanifested. If it has several duties to complete, and is to act as a life-long companion, choose a special phrase that will free it at the time of your death. Your elemental or pooka will then live on as an independent being, as long as its food supply lasts.

What food will your elemental or pooka eat? Due to its energetic constitution, your elemental or pooka needs to have some means for renewing its energy, especially if you have decided it will have a long life. It actually consumes energy. Your responsibility is to determine what will act as its basis of nourishment. You can arrange for your creature to live off of prana or etheric energy. This would guarantee a viable energy or food source for an extended, perhaps infinite, duration. You can choose several types of main courses for your creature, depending upon your needs and the uses for your elemental or pooka.

Next, define your creature's form or image. What does it look like? Does it resemble a fluffy cat, a golden dragon, or a sphere of white light? Allow yourself to conceive of its shape, whether unusual or common. Will your elemental or pooka be free to move about while resting or will it light in one specific place, such as a picture, statue, lamp, drawer, or trinket. What do you call your new creation? When you ascertain its name, you can summon it more easily. A name gives the elemental or pooka another dimension and more definition. If you have any problems identifying your creation, ask it to give you its name. Generally, they will respond quickly and concisely. After all, it exists to serve you and behaves accordingly.

Calculate exactly what duties you want your elemental or pooka to undertake on your behalf. Perhaps its purpose is to project or relate a sensation of love or sexual pleasure. You may choose to make an elemental to guard your home, or to bring more prosperity into your life. Be as clear and comprehensive as possible. An elemental makes an excellent assistant, whereas a pooka acts more as a friend and constant companion. Pookas evolve and have personalities, and often seem either female or male. Given enough time and energy, they can develop into tangible form with an individual mind. The pooka's potential reflects your intentions and expectations, and everything it comes in contact with or absorbs.

Your pooka will need a dwelling place. Its home can be in practically anything you choose, although common sense dictates certain guidelines. The object you choose should last as long as you use your pooka, and should conduct energy efficiently. Rings or amulets containing metal and stone make excellent homes for pookas. Mechanical objects, such as watches, should be avoided as the procedure often causes shifts in the magnetic field and can damage these items. Arrange your pooka program so your friend can come and go, at will, during slack times. Your pooka can learn and grow from these excursions.

After you carefully define the parameters of your ele-mental or pooka, you are ready to do the work. You must have an intense desire to induce a magical state. Move into a state of mind and being where you want this elemental or pooka more than anything else. Place all of your energy and concentration upon creating a perfect new being.

111

Your creature's power and abilities directly correlate to the depth of your merge. Boldly reach into the unmani-fested and bring a portion of it out. Take this force and fashion it in a manifest form, impressing this form with the parameters discussed previously. Actually see and feel yourself taking a sphere of unmanifest energy. Using your intent, mold this energy into your elemental or pooka. You may wish to stand in front of a mirror and see the unmanifest energy as if it were a shining ball of energy you are holding in your hands. Use the mirror to focus on shaping the energy until you are finished constructing your creature. If you make an error in the procedure, release the elemental or pooka and make a second effort. To release your elemental or pooka from its relationship with you, simply merge and let it go. Work with these techniques until you feel you have mastery over them.

Pookas and elementals can exist in other times and places. As you merge more deeply and frequently, you may find yourself existing in more than one time and space. Time may seem horizontal rather than linear, and you may discover the many worlds within your world. The implications are fascinating. Join us now for an adventure into just such an otherworld, complete with pookas and magical experiences.

Guided Journey: Lughnassad

At the close of a long summer day, just before the sun disappears behind the hills, she travels to her special place. The end of a flat rock juts out from the creek bank, providing the perfect spot to sit, relax, and reflect upon the infiniteness of oneness. In the winter, the creek fills with rain water, and the rocks make a small waterfall. But in the summer, the creek dries up, exposing the rock she calls her special place. In the creek bed she sits pressing bay leaves between her fingers. The fragrance overwhelms her, and sends her into a more relaxed, more aware, state of being.

Oaks heavy with mistletoe, madrone, and bay trees completely encircle the creek. Birds call to one another. The last remains of light ripple down through the leaves of the trees, casting interesting patterns of light and shadow.

She watches one particular pattern of light intently. The sunlight hits it then swirls, spins, and flows in all directions. Its brightness almost hurts her eyes as she shades them with her hand.

She moves toward the pattern of light which appears to be twenty feet down the creek bed. As she steps closer the light takes shape, and she realizes it is a beautiful diamond-like stone, embedded in the rock floor of the creek. She looks up and sees another stone down the creek bed. This one glows like the red ember of a fire. Soon she discovers a total of nine stones. Her discovery takes her further down the creek bed until the surroundings no longer look familiar.

The ninth stone is a clear crystal point, whose shape and clarity epitomize natural perfection. The only stone not embedded in rock, she picks up the point and holds it in her hand. Her fingers tingle and she feels a rush of energy quake through her body. She senses an importance in the crystal, and she places it in her pocket.

She hears splashing water, and looks up to see a pool of water down from where she found the crystal.

"That's odd," she says aloud. "I didn't realize there was any water in the creek this time of year."

As she moves closer to the pool of water, she notices it is a beautiful and distinctive color of blue. The color is odd, not a hue one would forget. Staring into the water, she sees the reflection of an unfamiliar face. The features appear smaller, and the face narrower and elfin-like. The lips move, but she can't hear what he is saying. She senses that he is beckoning to her to follow him.

Suddenly, the image of the elf transforms into the reflection of a crystal rose. The petals of the rose stretch out most of the way across the pool. A slight breeze sends ripples through the rose. A point of light begins in the middle of the rose, and spreads outward until the whole rose is on fire. She stares deeper and deeper into the rose until she feels consumed by the light.

Everything swirls and her senses feel like that of a cat, relaxed, but keenly aware of her surroundings. Dimensional boundaries fall away as she moves like light through time, space, and energy. She feels like a feather carried by the breeze, gently settling back to earth.

She feels the firmness of the earth beneath her feet and hears the sound of voices all around her. She looks around to see that she is on a dirt path with many other beings. The setting sun appears before her. The sky becomes alive with a vast array of color, like a palette of paint spilled and dripped with intention.

In the middle of the sunset stands a city. The city looks like a crown of jewels brought to life by the rays of the sun. Everyone on the path, including herself, moves toward the city. She notices the movement does not appear mechanical, but instead bubbles with laughter, song, and a genuine love of life. The feeling catches like wildfire, and soon she finds herself singing and dancing with all around her. It feels like a celebration.

She touches the being in front of her on the back to ask him about the celebration. He turns toward her, and she sees that it is the elfin face that she saw in the pool of water. For a moment, she becomes speechless, but soon regains her composure and tongue.

"Is this a celebration, and if so, what celebration is it?" she finally asks.

"Before us lies the City of Charis, and we are all going there to celebrate the festival of Lughnassad," the elf replies in a sing-song voice that is sweet and velvety.

"What is Lughnassad?" she asks without hesitation.

"Have you not heard of the god Lugh?" he asks with amazement in his voice. Before waiting for her to reply, he begins again, "Why Lugh is the most handsome of men, a great artist, a fine horsemen, and I hear tell a most magnificent lover. The word 'nassad' means 'to give in marriage.'"

"Oh, I see. Lughnassad must be a celebration of the marriage of Lugh," she interrupts. "Who is he marrying?"

The elf smiles before answering her question. "He marries Rosemerta, a beautiful maiden whose love every man longs for, and the wife every man wishes was his." With this last line, the elf is swept along by the crowd moving toward the city. She pauses for a moment before proceeding in the direction of Charis and the marriage feast of Lugh and Rosemerta.

Along the road, she meets an old man with long white hair and beard. He is gentle and friendly, and she walks along with him for a while on their way to the city and the festival. He pulls her aside for a moment and shows her his pooka, a golden dragon. She watches as the dragon does somersaults in the air before landing on her shoulder.

"He seems to like you," chuckles the old man. "Would you like to learn how to make your own pooka?"

She nods at him with excited anticipation.

"Do you have anything, like a piece of jewelry or something, that we could put the pooka in? My pooka lives in my ring." He holds up his right hand, exposing a ring on his index finger. The stone shines fiery red much like the red stone she saw back in the creek bed.

"I don't have any jewelry with me," she replies while searching through her pockets. A bulge in her pocket reveals the crystal point she found in the creek bed. Pulling it out, she hands the point to the old man.

"Perfect," he says, holding the crystal up to the light of the sun. "Pookas are energetic beings that feed off of pure energy. They can be programmed to do a number of things. Do you know what you want to program it for?"

She looks at him pensively and asks, "What can I program a pooka for?"

"You can program them for protection, spiritual guidance, or to read patterns. The possibilities are only limited by your own mind."

Suddenly an idea occurs to her. "I'd like to program the pooka to help me access my artistic self."

"Stare into the crystal, directing your mind to create a pooka which will live in the crystal and guide you in your artistic exploration. Allow yourself to live your dream," he says in a raised voice.

She watches as white light explodes in the tip of the crystal, then runs down the sides like melting ice cream, until finally streams of colored light pour out through the base of the crystal. She hears the crystal vibrate. The tone begins low, but steadily rises in pitch until it sounds like a high, fast pulsing in her head. Abruptly the vibrations cease, and the light emanating from the crystal is a sparkle. The old man hands her the crystal.

117

"Merry meet, merry part," he whispers in her ear before turning and disappearing into the crowd of people.

Immediately, the crystal feels warm and alive. She senses the creature who now lives in the crystal. It reminds her of a cat, agile and sleek. She holds the crystal and begins to walk toward the city and the celebration of Lughnassad. Overhead a mighty hawk flies past holding a serpent in its sharp talons. Music and song erupt all around her. Her feet begin to dance. She has no control.

Further down the path, she stops and watches a spider spin its web. It is the image of the goddess, renewing the cycle of life from the well of creation.

"Hello," echoes a man's voice, startling her from thought. She raises her head and looks into the man's eyes. They are the same color as the pool back at the creek bed. She feels a hand energetically touch her, showering light from her to the young man and back again.

A voice whispers, "He's the one."

The feeling of knowing she has with him transcends time and space. She continues to stare deep within the pools of his eyes. He stares back into the green forest of her eyes. The energy between them feels like a bond renewed, a bond of oneness between two beings of energy. She feels his hand in hers, fingers penetrating fingers. Together they dance toward the city.

Moving closer to the city gate, the excitement intensifies. The gate is made of two giant standing stones with a third giant stone perched on top of the other two. In front of the standing stones are two immense stone cats guarding the entrance to the city. She feels a rush of energy as she enters the gate. She realizes she has walked through a portal. The city is cast in translucent red light. She notices that the light reflects the red sun shining on the horizon. All the people seem to be moving toward a big hall with massive spires that rests in the center of the city.

Soon, the man and woman stand hand in hand in the great hall. All around them, people are either waiting for the wedding or preparing for it. She can feel the anticipation mounting in the air as the moment of the marriage of Lugh and Rosemerta draws ever closer.

She hears the murmur of the crowd and turns to her left. She sees the bride wearing a white wedding gown and flowers in her hair, waiting for the procession to the altar.

But wait, this does not look like Rosemerta! The bride's face is old and weathered, like that of a crone. The ladies in waiting drape the veil over the bride's face.

At the ancient stone altar stands a young man with his back to the crowd. He looks of average height, but his muscles are lithe and agile like those of a mountain lion. A red glow surrounds him. The cacophony of the crowd suddenly turns into one tone, like a meditative Om. From this note, music begins to spring to life from every dimension. Music completely fills the senses.

The bride and groom stand with their backs to the crowd, as the High Priest solemnizes the wedding vows. His voice rings out, "Daughter, it is said of the goddess that thou art every wife and every wife art thou. Do you seek this union with the full knowledge of its sacred nature?"

The woman answers, "Yes, blessed be!"

The High Priestess, standing next to the High Priest, looks at the groom and recites, "My son, it is said of the god that thou art every husband and every husband art thou! Do you seek this union with the full knowledge of its sacred nature?"

The man answers with a smile in his eyes, "Yes, blessed be!"

The High Priestess brings the marriage box from the altar, and stands next to the High Priest, holding it open in her hands while he asks, "My son and my daughter, show us the symbols which you have brought today as a pledge of your love."

The groom carefully places a smooth white pebble, three silver coins, and a small bundle of seven woods in the ornate box. The bride lays a small white feather, a bag of seeds, and a packet with seven different spices on top of his objects.

The High Priest addresses the wedding couple, "My son and my daughter, show all who are here your true intent with the yarns of union." The man then ties a knot around a piece of green yarn that the bride is holding out, and she in turn ties a knot around his red yarn.

The High Priest continues, "Before the goddess and her consort, and all who are gathered here, you have shown us your true intent. Now make your pledge."

The High Priestess holds the marriage box forward. The man, who has retained the yarn, places it in the box and the woman takes the box and slowly closes the lid. The High Priest puts his hand on the woman's head and the High Priestess puts her hand on the man's head. Together they say, "In the name of the gods, we bless this union!"

The bride and groom reply, "Blessed be! Blessed be our union! Praise be to the gods!"

Everyone in the hall happily shouts in unison, "Blessed Be!" Lugh and Rosemerta turn to face the crowd.

First, the woman sees that Lugh is the man with eyes like the pool in the creek bed. She then sees that as the bride's veil is lifted, that it is no longer the crone's face she saw before, but her own! The man kisses her and bells begin to ring. The crowd roars its approval, and the feast begins.

After much merriment and celebration, she feels her lover tug gently at her arm. She sees his playful smile and she knows his desire. He gathers her into his arms and carries her up a staircase leading to a second story.

As they reach the top, the hall vanishes into dust and the two of them lay naked in the soft grass next to the creek bed. She feels his body pressed against hers. Sensual waves of desire echo through her body, caressing her womanhood.

In the moon's reflection, her lover's face shines brightly. She studies the lines of his face, touching each one with the tip of her fingers, slowly and sensually.

He touches her gently and looks into the face of the goddess. His rough fingers brush the back of her neck, and her hair stands on end. The woman shivers involuntarily. She feels the heat of his touch move over her skin, like wildfire. The man kisses her thoroughly and moves over her. He moves into her like the setting sun moves down into the horizon, soft and slow.

The creek courses once again, the water flowing by the lovers as they join as one.

᪥

CHAPTER SEVEN

Hellith's Day

Triana & Hellith

The winter winds whisper in the distance
Burnt orange and red hues of remembering
Night comes quietly riding the evening sun
The dark warmth reminds me of you.

❧ Hellith's Day ❧

Triana & Hellith

The element is water

The Goddess and Her Consort

The sound of baying hounds coming over the hills heralds the Autumn Equinox and Hellith's Day, the seventh Great Day on the path of the sun. Like Lughnassad, Hellith's Day is associated with death. The male consort Hellith symbolizes the dying sun. The word "hell" stems from the root of this god's name. The negative aspects of this word stem from religious politics, but the ancient Gwyddons considered hell or "hel" as primarily an otherworld, rather than a place of punishment. In Teutonic mythology, hell was the realm of nine worlds under the roots of Yggdrasil, and was inhabited by those who died of disease or old age. Hellith's Day marks the harvest. Traditional celebrations are still observed in parts of rural Britain. Everyone participates in the festivities on the last day of bringing the harvest home. Other names used for Hellith's Day are the Ingathering or Inning. In Scotland, this ritual day is called the Kern.

❧
125

The festivities of Hellith's Day begin after sunset on the eve of the Great Day. The ritual is brief, ending in:

Come dance with us and we will dance with you.

At this point, members dance a spiral dance with hands linked together, very carefully and slowly, exaggerating each step. No sounds are uttered during the beginning of the dance. When sufficient tension builds, the members bay like the hounds of death, louder and louder, dancing ever faster. The feast follows the dance, with merriment and light-hearted conversation.

The consort Hellith is an aspect of Kernunnos. The natural progression of the sun parallels the faces of the consort. Kernunnos is Tarvos. Tarvos transforms into Belenus. Belenus becomes Lugh, and Lugh makes way for Hellith. Hellith then evolves into Esus, the lord of destruction and death. Hellith is a god of the dying sun, and if invoked, he brings peace and tranquility to people approaching death. Souls belong in his protection until they reach their destination, Tir-nan-Og.

The goddess knows Hellith as a loving and gentle consort. He plays a magical flute that brings peace to anyone who hears it, and holds a disc of the setting sun in his hands. He appears as all ages, and has pale blonde or reddish hair. Often, Hellith wears robes that blend with his eyes, hair, and skin. One face of the consort looks like the red embers of a dying bonfire.

The Threefold Mother, Triana, is Hellith's mate. She manifests as goddess of the sun, earth, and moon, and represents the oneness of birth, life, and death. As Sun-Ana, she is a goddess of healing, knowledge, and powers of the mind. She appears in a white robe with a brilliant golden mantle, clasped together at her breast with the emblem of a sun disc. As Earth-Ana, she wears green robes with a brown mantle clasped together with a copper broach, fashioned as three leaves from green metal. Earth-Ana symbolizes nature, life, and death. Moon-Ana is a goddess of higher love and complete wisdom. She appears in a gray robe held together at her breast by a silver crescent moon.

Triana acts as a goddess of discipline and diplomacy. She teaches the skills of tact and ecological demeanor. The goddess is ageless. Her three aspects denote the maid, mother, and crone. Her presence seems all-pervasive and universally wise. Triana holds the Great Book of knowledge in her hands and gives answers to those who ask.

The goddess Triana and her consort Hellith symbolize aspects of the cycle. What does "symbolize" mean? A symbol stands for or represents something. We use symbols to communicate on a daily basis. They are so strongly ingrained in our culture that we rarely notice how frequently we use them. Symbols and concepts are cornerstones in all magic, and give greater depth to the patterns we create.

Practical Knowledge and Useful Information—Patterns in Magic, Perception, and Views

Symbolism occurs with the process of association. Your mind uses symbols and symbolism to arouse these associations so that an attitude or concept is suggested or encompassed by a word, song, sign, gesture, body position, dream, object, animal, food, or picture. Symbols and symbolism represent collections or quantums of thought, feeling, or sensation. All things that exist in the manifest have some degree of symbolism and association.

Symbols and symbolism convey an aura of feeling and thinking which coalesces a range of ideas, or forms a framework of context. Symbols and symbolism have a layered quality. One thing gives meaning to another, with personal experience adding another valence to symbolic representations. Symbolic association stretches the capacity of thought and expression, and becomes a channel through which universal and elemental concepts are conveyed. Symbolism goes beyond definition and moves into magical dimensions.

The human mind has two primary ways of differentiating symbols and their associations. The first uses logic, the part of your mind that communicates by numbers and words. The second way uses a holistic and conceptual system to convey meanings. This creative part of your mind surpasses cause and effect and identifies concepts as a whole, without separation. This area of your mind is the part that merges with the boundless.

Integrating and using both areas of your mind is essential when doing magical works. Logic gives structure, and creativity allows you to merge. These two avenues of your mind are symbiotic, meaning they work together cooperatively and depend on one another.

When you do any work of magic, you use the Three Eyes of Kerridwen (expectation, desire, and merging). Expectation and desire join the creative and logical areas of your mind, using symbol and symbolism. This gives you a groundwork from which to merge. When you merge, you structure energy in the manifest and unmanifest. Logic and form open the door to the boundless, which has no doors. Viewed as an abstract and seen symbolically, this concept makes perfect sense.

All magic flows from the integration of these symbiotic areas of your mind. Symbols and symbolism are the language of the goddess and her consort. The greater your knowledge of the feeling and history behind symbolism and associations, the stronger your rapport with the goddess and the god. You can speak their language symbolically using several different modes of sensory awareness.

Patterning magic uses five basic modes, one for each of the fives senses: visual, kinesthetic, auditory, gustatory, and olfactory. Add to these modes as you master energetic patterning.

The visual mode includes anything you perceive with your eyes. Employing light, color, shapes, graphics, patterns and textures in your magical works gives you a visual platform from which to cross over to the world of the goddess and her consort. One of the more effective ways you can use the sight mode involves the application of geometrical shapes. This method is employed in Gwyddonic tradition as well as by the Tibetan, Indian, and Buddhist cultures. These geometrical patterns are called mandalas.

Mandalas are generally comprised of a geometrical pattern of lines and shapes and colors with particular meaning. Each part of the mandala has its own meaning. Joined together into this one form, the meanings become one meaning—a symbol, a representation, and a means of linking with the boundless. Expectation and desire, the first two eyes of Kerridwen, are conveyed in the mandala. By merging with the symbol, you immediately move into oneness, where you can then bring about that which you expect and desire.

The kinesthetic mode utilizes the sensation of touch and feeling and applies to sexual expression, movement, and gestures. The guided journeys make special use of kinesthetic associations. Your body has memory and several different levels of awareness. Sexual expression containing a positive expectation and desire almost always results in a satisfying and enjoyable merging experience.

The auditory mode affects you through sound. Singing, chanting, music, drumming, ringing bells, sighing, moaning, wailing, and even the rhythmic sound of breathing can assist you in successful magical works.

The gustatory mode is significant in ritual and celebrations. Food and drink often have specialized associative meanings. Drinking wine represents more than just the beverage. Wine depicts the blood of life and rebirth. Eating or drinking particular substances brings that symbolic energy inside your body. Each kind of food has a different effect on your body, mind, and spirit. Certain foods can help facilitate your magical experience.

The olfactory mode employs smell and scent to move you to a magical place or altered state. Perfumes, incense, potpourri, flowers, plants, and other fragrant items can be used alone or layered with the other patterning modes. The more layering of modes in your patterning, both in your everyday life and in your magical world, the stronger your patterns. Mastering the modes gives mastery over patterning. All magic is done by patterning.

Symbolism and association create an expansive perception of the world. They allow many ideas, thoughts, feelings, and experiences to be conveyed by one thing. Communication in this conceptual and symbolic fashion actually alters your perception, which in turn, changes very real constructs of your reality. If you have constructed a rigid reality, it may be more difficult to understand and incorporate symbolic meanings. A flexible view gives you much more freedom to express and experience life. Flexibility in this case does not mean being impractical or irresponsible, but rather, having the ability to shift perspective.

You may ask, "How many views are there?" William Blake explains, "If the doors of perception were cleansed, then all would be as it is, infinite." Our desires are limited by our perceptions. You cannot desire what you have not perceived, yet our ability to perceive is infinite. When you view reality as an infinite creation, you are seeing the world with the eyes of the goddess and her consort. The boundless is infinite. Oneness is an open set and everything is possible. Limitation ceases to exist.

You view things with your mind, memory, and body. To view your world without distortion simplifies and clarifies everything. Your conditioning shapes and colors your viewing lens, often to such a degree that your reality becomes burdened with connotation. One method for letting go of this connotation and distortion is to take on many different views, moving from one to the other without emotional or intellectual attachment. This gives you a broader base to work from when you pattern in magic. Your awareness and personal development grow in leaps and bounds when you apply this technique. See the world through your partner's, parents', or friend's eyes. See the world from a tree's view, a dragonfly's view, or an eagle's view. Try on another culture and see how it feels. What is your perception of the world from that viewpoint?

Your view and perceptions shape your world. Gwyddonic magic is based on the premise that you have the capacity within yourself to harness and direct every force in nature, and to affect every energetic particle and wave in the cosmos. For example, you have probably changed your mind, or your view, at some point in your life. Deepak Chopra writes, "If I can change my mind, and if the world is made of the same stuff as my mind, then I can change the world."

Absolutely everyone and everything you come in contact with alters your view. Moment by moment, your perception is ever-changing, adapting, and developing in infinite directions. Remember, one person's metaphysical truth is another person's conditioned reality. Your view is just that—your view. A strong and clear perception leads to strong and clear patterns. When your patterns are

131

strong and viable, it becomes much easier to ecologically design your world. Mind views and mind moves. Mind patterns and mind merges. Your perceptions really are all in your mind.

Understand that awareness floods inward and outward to create your perceptions. Nietzsche said, "All philosophy is based upon the premise that we think, but it is equally possible that we are being thought." Everything that exists is a movement or transformation of mind space from one guise to another. People, animals, mountains, valleys, oceans, and universes are continually being thought and perceived.

Chopra states, "A glance is behaving as a carrier wave, transmitting mental intention out into the world and placing it upon whatever is being observed. Instead of understanding visual perception as a taking in of reality, this viewpoint, which was shared by Aristotle and the entire ancient world, says that perception confers reality. The same holds true for the other senses." Interestingly, most primitive people believe that when you look at an object or person, the mind flows out through your eyes. Sight is explained as light moving in, and mind moving out.

Your world reflects your view. But how many views can you maintain at one time? Through effort and practice, you can learn to perceive several different worlds at one time. A strong expectation of success, a desire to experience these infinite views, and a deep merge are your tickets to an exciting and expansive framework from which to pattern your world(s). The implication here is that you construct your realities, shape your quest, and choose your birth, life, and death. Everything stems from your level of awareness.

Learn to shift your awareness and view your reality through romance and sexual expression. Romance fills your life because that is your perception and choice. You participate in creating your world. You are the artist. A pleasurable and satisfying sexual life becomes real because that is your perception. So pattern accordingly and choose your view. Your ultimate experience becomes simply a matter of turning your mind to oneness and allowing for the boundless possibilities. Merge and enjoy yourself.

Guided Journey: Hellith's Day

The lady walks through the forest holding a palette of paint. Everywhere she goes, she splashes color. More vivid than any painting, the ground and the trees are alive with shades of red, green, and gold. She takes a deep breath and exhales slowly. She notices that the air has a slight chill to it. She closes her eyes and listens to the leaves whispering in the autumn breeze.

For a moment, she becomes a leaf. She imagines herself changing color to vibrant red, then letting go of the tree that she had been hanging onto all spring and summer. She feels herself floating toward the ground like a feather, gliding back and forth. Just as she is about to touch the ground, she feels the breeze lift her up toward the tops of the trees.

She floats high above the forest, becoming more relaxed and aware. The clouds caress her skin with sensation, and she feels like a girl in a swing, flying naked and free. She sees a flock of ducks stretching out across the sky in the shape of a giant "V," moving south for the winter. She feels the warmth of the sun, and wonders how much higher she can go.

Down in the forest below, she sees a small clearing. She begins to float down toward the opening, rocking slowly back and forth as she descends through the air. The clearing appears to grow as she moves closer. She can now start to make out definite shapes moving below.

The clearing appears to be perfectly round, surrounded by trees on all sides. She sees shadows moving about within the circle. She senses that it is a gathering of some kind. A bright light seems to be coming from the middle of the clearing, but she still cannot make out where it is coming from. She hovers fifty feet above the clearing, and then gradually moves down.

She can now see shadowy shapes dressed in forest green robes. On one side of the clearing is a table covered with food. As she moves closer, she sees that the light from the center of the circle shines from a giant crystal obelisk. The obelisk reflects the rays of the sun, filling the entire circle with its light. She feels the ground under her feet, and realizes that she has landed on one side of the clearing. The people do not seem to notice her as they continue their preparation for the festivities.

Finally, a young man comes over to greet her. He holds a goblet of wine in his hand. He kisses her on the cheek and hands her the silver rune-marked goblet.

"Merry meet, merry part," he whispers in her ear. "Drink from the greeting cup."

She takes a sip from the goblet. The wine tastes faintly sweet. She hands it back to the young man, who then stands back from her and with a smile says, "Blessed be all who enter our circle."

He then takes her by the hand, and steers her toward the rest of the gathering. "We are so happy you could make it. We've been expecting you."

She looks at him with astonishment, but at the same time she has a knowing in her heart and mind. It feels much like coming home. With that thought, she feels a rush of energy and light flood her body and flow into her head.

The young man introduces her to the others at the gathering. Everywhere smiling faces and warm voices repeat, "Merry meet and merry part. The perfect love of the goddess, and the perfect peace of the god." Now she knows she has come home.

After meeting everyone gathered, the young man directs her to a place just outside the circle under a tree. "Please wait here until I come for you," he says firmly. She nods in acknowledgement. He turns and walks back to the gathering in the circle. She watches from outside.

In the distance she hears dogs barking. It is the sound of baying hounds coming over the hills in the far distance. She feels a cold shiver, and knows the time is near. Off on the right, away from the circle, through the trees she sees a golden bull as he dances and prances through the forest. By his side are three gray cranes. Each of them knows the answer as they dance and prance through the woods. The smell of the damp earth and the faint scent of amber fill her senses.

The young man returns, holding a cup in one hand and a leather cord and a blindfold in the other. He sets the cup down next to her, before taking both her wrists and tying them together. He then picks up the cup and hands it to her. It is filled with a dark, foul-smelling liquid.

"The liquid in this cup symbolizes your conditioning, and the death of your old self. Drink it so that you may be free of your conditioning and ready for your rebirth," he says softly but firmly. She drinks the liquid from the cup, grimacing at the bitter taste. He then blindfolds her, takes both her hands, and guides her to the North point of the circle.

"Who goes there?" booms a voice in front of her. "Who is it that comes to this earthen gate? I, the Warden of the Gates demand to know."

From beside her, she hears the young man answer the voice, "It is I, the Hound of Annwn, who is the guide of souls, that stands before thy gate."

"Who is that with you?" inquires the booming voice.

"It is a lost and wandering soul that I have guided here," replies the young man.

"Oh soul, what do you seek here?"

A moment of silence prevails before she realizes the Warden is now speaking to her. She gropes for words but finds none. Suddenly, a whisper from the young man directs her to say, "I, a wandering and lost soul, do seek entrance to the Castle of Glass, that there I may learn the secrets of control over all material and physical things."

"What is the password? You may not enter unless you know it," bellows the Warden.

"I know it, but I cannot remember it!" she responds. "Pray, let me enter anyway."

"Nay! I cannot! Depart from here and seek elsewhere."

The Hound then escorts her to the West point.

The Warden asks, "Who goes there? Who is it that comes to this watery gate? I, the Warden of the Gates, demand to know."

The young man replies, "It is I, the Hound of Death, the guide of souls, who stands before your gate."

"Who is that with you?" the Warden inquires.

"It is a lost and wandering soul that I have guided here."

The Warden asks again, "Wandering soul, what do you seek here?"

She hears the whisper in her ear and responds, "I, a wandering and lost soul, do seek entrance to the Castle of the Lady of the Lake, that there I may learn the secret of control over all emotions, feelings, and desires."

The Warden questions, "What is the password? You may not enter unless you know it."

"I know it, but I cannot remember it. Pray, let me enter anyway."

"No, I cannot! Depart from here and seek elsewhere," the Warden tells her.

The Hound spins her around in several circles and then conducts her counterclockwise to the South point where the Warden calls out, "Who goes there? Who is it that comes to this fiery gate? I, the Warden of the Gates, demand to know."

"It is I, the Hound of Pwyll, the guide of souls, who stands before your gate."

"Who is that with you?"

"It is a lost and wandering soul I have guided here."

The Warden inquires, "Oh soul, what do you seek here?"

Again she hears the faint voice in her ear, and replies, "I, a wandering and lost soul, do seek entrance to the Castle of Fire that there I may learn the secrets of control over all forms of energy and power."

"What is the password? You may not enter unless you know it!" booms the strong voice of the Warden.

"I know it, but I cannot remember it! Pray, let me enter anyway," she pleads. She is disoriented and her wrists feel sore from being tied together.

The Warden answers, "No, I cannot! Depart from here and seek elsewhere."

The Hound spins her around once again and then leads her to the East point.

"Who goes there? Who is it that comes to this windy gate? I, the Warden of the Gates, demand to know."

She hears the young man answer, "It is I, the Hound of Nodens, the guide of souls, who stands before your gate."

"Who is that with you?"

"It is a lost and wandering soul I have guided here."

The voice of the Warden asks once again, "Oh soul, what do you seek here?"

She hears the whisper and repeats, "I, a wandering and lost soul, do seek entrance to the Castle of the Winds that I may learn the great wisdom that gives control over all things, whatsoever they may be."

The Warden asks again for the password. She realizes what it is, and blurts out, "I know it! It is perfect love and perfect peace! Now, let me enter."

The warden answers warmly, "You do know it, but because you do not know its meaning you may not enter in at this gate. But do not despair, you may enter in at the Little Gate for those who seek to learn the ancient wisdom."

She feels a hand on her back moving her down into a crouch. She crawls through the Little Gate, through the parted legs of a woman, into the circle.

"Welcome! You have come a long way! Come kneel before me and I will tell you the true meaning of the password 'perfect love and perfect peace.'" She kneels before the Warden.

He continues, "First, it means the perfect love of the goddess, and the perfect peace of the god. Second, it means the perfect love of knowledge and the perfect peace of wisdom. Third, it means the perfect love of all nature and the perfect peace by being in harmony with all things, whether animate or inanimate."

The young man removes her blindfold before the Warden recites the oath of initiation. She repeats it clearly and the cord, binding her hands, is then cut.

"What name have you taken?" asks the Warden.

"Greenfire," she replies without hesitation.

"I, Hellith, High Priest of this gathering declare before the ancient gods that Greenfire is a true Gwyddon. So mote it be!" He then puts a crystal necklace around her porcelain neck and traces a star with a circle around it, with scented oil on her forehead.

"Rise, Greenfire, and receive the blessing and consecration of the gods." He crosses his wand and athame together, and tells her to take hold of them. He instructs her to take in as much power and blessing as she can hold without passing out. He then hugs and kisses her, and welcomes her into the group. The others embrace and welcome her.

The feast begins, and lasts the rest of the day. An abundance of food and drink satiates everyone's appetites.

At one point an older woman dressed in a sheaf of corn, together with her consort, are drenched by a bucket of water. The young man tells her that the old woman symbolizes the corn mother, and her consort is called the reaper. The corn mother symbolizes the abundance of the harvest, and gives thanks to the gods. All day, they sing and dance and explore the woods.

As the sun sets peacefully in the western sky, the young man beckons her to follow him. After saying good-bye to everyone, he leads her out of the circle and into the forest.

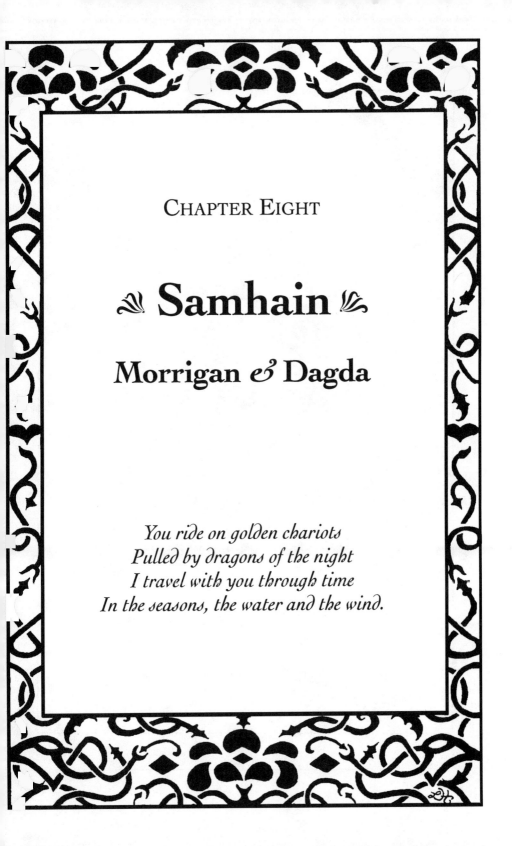

CHAPTER EIGHT

❧ Samhain ☙

Morrigan & Dagda

You ride on golden chariots
Pulled by dragons of the night
I travel with you through time
In the seasons, the water and the wind.

CHAPTER EIGHT

Samhain

Morrigan & Dagda

The element is halfway between water and earth

The Goddess and Her Consort

Falling at the beginning of November, the Samhain ritual takes place on the eve of the Great Day, designating the beginning of winter. The word literally means "the end of summer." Samhain is celebrated after sunset, and it is associated with the sleeping earth goddess. The ritual signifies the death of all things, and a time ruled by the dark goddess and her consort.

On Samhain, six months after Beltane, the veil between time and space draws to its thinnest point. This means that the spirits of the departed more easily communicate with the living on the eve of Samhain. The portals to other worlds open, and the goddess and her consort interact freely with humankind. Stories tell of people who pass through the portals into Tir-nan-Og. Some have returned to tell their tales. In Ireland, all the faery hills are thrown wide open and the faeries come forth. Anyone bold enough can visit for a while with them. If you do, you may not return until the next year on Samhain.

On Samhain Eve, messages from the goddess and gods and from the dead are conveyed to those who gather. By drawing lots, an individual is chosen to serve as the Oracle of Death. In a dark and quiet location, the Oracle merges with the unmanifested and answers your personal questions about the future. Each practitioner has a private session.

The Dumb Supper serves as another traditional observance on Samhain Eve. Generous plates of food and drink are placed outside in the dark of night, with lighted red and white candles standing guard. Any morsels or drops that remain the next morning go into the earth and to the goddess.

The great sea mother Morrigan makes love with the master of life and death, the Dagda, on the feast of Samhain. The feast marks the time when Tarvos, the golden one, is slain and goes to the land of the queen of those who die. Kerridwen, the All Mother, shows us a sprig of holly with red berries as a sign of her son's return.

The goddess Morrigan is a wise woman who portrays an aspect of the mother of the Tuatha, Danu. She is tall and regal as a queen of the sea. She wears a magical tiara of gold, silver, and pearl, and her robes are deep sea blues and greens, often tied with a white or shell pink cord. She smells of the sea, the sand, and thunderstorms. The beautiful goddess appears with silver-streaked hair, dark sea-green eyes, and opalescent skin. She holds the queen's rod of command and collects sand dollars. Often she is associated with ocean vegetation, manta rays, dolphins, and whales.

Morrigan parallels the Irish goddess, Morrigu, as a queen of death, life, and magic. Morrigu protects sailors and the shores of Erin. Like Morrigan, Morrigu (also called the Dark Gray Lady) represents the qualities of the sea and its contrasts of calm placidness and raging storminess.

On Samhain Morrigan takes Dagda, the good god, as her lover. As chief of the Tuatha De Danann, Dagda fathers the fire goddess Bridget and the consort, Angus Og. Lord of complete knowledge and dispenser of plenty, Dagda, the wise consort, appears with dark brown eyes and dark hair. He has a strong and manly body, and smells of rivers, the earth, and forests. He holds himself like a king, and wears royal blues and purples. The flesh hook and rods of command are his magical tools, along with the harp, the sword, and the cauldron.

As the creator and great father, Dagda possesses an inexhaustible cauldron from the mythical city of Murias. The cauldron is one of the four great treasures of the Tuatha De Danann. The consort also has ever-laden fruit trees and two marvelous swine; one that is always cooking, and one that never dies. Associated with oak trees, the Dagda traditionally has power over milk and corn.

Named for his prowess, the consort owns a great club which kills with one end and revives the dead with the other. In the Battle of Mag Tured, the Dagda kills uncountable Fomorians. The Fomorians are mythologically associated with the forces of nature which challenge humankind, like winter. Wherever his spear trails on the ground, a deep ditch marks the earth. When the Dagda, Lugh, and Ogmios go into the Fomorian's camp to rescue his harper, Dagda sees his harp hanging on the wall and he invokes it. The harp flies into his hand, killing nine Fomorians as it passes. He then plays the Three Strains— the Strain of Sorrowing, the Strain of Laughter, and the Strain of Sleep. The last tune puts the Fomorians to sleep, and the Dagda, with Lugh and Ogmios, leave the camp unchallenged. After the battle, Dagda divides the hills and mounds of Ireland among the Tuatha De Danann.

Your experiences with Morrigan and the Dagda increase your knowledge and understanding of the attributes and aspects they represent. You can incorporate these qualities in yourself, using the energy for magical patterns. Morrigan may impart her wisdom to you, and her consort Dagda may show you the rods of power and command made of golden metals, crystal, and wood.

Rapport with Morrigan strengthens as you move closer to the ocean. The Dagda is often seen by rivers, by mighty oaks, and in the dream world. The ritual of feasting honors the Great Father, satiating his prodigious appetite. Much like the goddess, the consort serves as a patron god of the druids and is credited with great wisdom and an expansive mind. As the mighty one of all knowledge, Dagda is fondly called Ruadh Rofhessa.

Practical Knowledge and Useful Information— Dragons and Dragon Veins

The wisdom attributed to the goddess and her consort carries over to the animal world. The magical dragon is also considered a great being of wisdom and knowledge. The dragon, like the goddess and her consort, knows the secrets of renewal and perpetual rebirth. Like the All Mother and All Father, the dragon defies the limitations of the natural world.

The dragon has its roots in ancient female deities who were deposed by a new order of sky-gods. The greatest of these deities, the Mother of us all, took for herself two aspects: one which we call the Bright One and the other which we call the Dark One—symbols of manifest and unmanifest energies. This signifies an ever-renewing of all things, that all things might ever grow, learning from what has passed before.

The Bright One took upon herself three aspects, and likewise did she who is Dark. Because of this, all things whether bright or dark, have a beginning, middle, and end; youth, middle age, and old; positive, neutral, and negative; birth, life, and death. The goddess governs all things in this manner—dormant, the greening, and harvest. Before the coming of the sky-gods, she portrayed the sun and moon, but now she is only the moon. But to some, she still symbolizes all things.

The goddess typifies manifest energy while the dragon generally symbolizes unmanifested power. Newman, in *The Hill of the Dragon*, writes about the marriage of the dragon or the serpent to the Mother. He tells of a song sung to the goddess on Bridget's Fire.

> *Early on Bride's morn*
> *The serpent shall come from the hole,*
> *I will not molest the serpent,*
> *Nor will the serpent molest me.*
> *The serpent will come from the hole*
> *On the brown day of Bride.*
> *Though there be three feet of snow*
> *On the flat surface of the ground.*

The emergence of the serpent from the ground symbolizes life waking from its winter sleep, the unmanifest arising from the manifest Mother. By sowing the dragon's teeth, the manifest springs forth.

Dragon and serpent myths closely relate to the goddess tradition. Dragons pertain to ancestor worship and fertility. Traditionally, the blood of a dragon contains many marvelous properties. A bath of dragon's blood restores the petrified to life.

The Gundestrup cauldron depicts Kernunnos holding a serpent in his left hand, representing the unmanifest. He grasps a torque in his right hand, representing the manifest and associated with the path of the sun. Kernunnos is often pictured with a ram-horned serpent encircling his waist. The serpent belt acts as the god's sacred amulet, representing strength in battle and mastery over death. Kernunnos and the serpent are on intimate terms, as he would be with a close friend.

The serpent and dragon relate to fertility, with obvious phallic characteristics. Serpent worship was transformed into sun worship. In Britain, a Gaulish tribe called the Belgae carved the hillside form known as the Cerne Giant. Older forms of the word are *Kern* or *Kern-El,* which means "hill of the solar deity, Bel."

The alchemical dragon acts as guardian and the personification of spiritual transcendence. The dragon identifies himself as Mercurius, a super-refined type of quicksilver known as philosopher's mercury and identified with the Spirit of God. This substance represents the unity of all diversity where female and male powers of earth and heaven reconcile. The common alchemical symbol for this is the Uroboros, a serpent or dragon biting its own tale and signifying that All is One.

The Chinese regard the dragon as beneficial, a regal and exalted life-giving deity commanding veneration and homage. The dragon is a fertilizing symbol representing the regenerative processes underlying the cosmic scheme. Philosophers like Confucius use the dragon to explain the nature of things. He states, "Things that accord in tone vibrate together. Things that have affinity in their inmost natures seek one another. Water flows to what is wet, fire turns to what is dry. Clouds (the breath of heaven) follow the dragon, wind (the breath of earth) follows the tiger."

In China, the dragon animates the countryside and appears as twisting currents of energy irrigating the rocky hills and lands. In the winter, this force is dormant. With the advent of summer, the power expresses its qualities in the vivid rhythms of the quickening earth. The exhalations of the dragon's breath form the clouds, bringing the rain. The magical creature represents a powerful water god who can magically shrink into a raindrop. The dragon is almost always associated with water in some manner. In contrast, the creature also breathes fire, which symbolizes the lightning that illuminates the sky—arousing and inspiring.

Folklore of the Old World and the new frequently references the dragon. The ancient ones saw the dragon among the stars, calling the mighty one, Draco, a circumpolar constellation of the northern sky. Four thousand years ago the yellow star Thuban, in the tail of Draco, was the pole star to which the slanting shaft in the Great Pyramid of Khufu at Gizeh was oriented.

As the guardian of the goddess' treasures, the dragon presides over the mountains and the dragon veins that form a patterned network over the surface of the globe. These dragon veins resemble the meridian lines used in the ancient Chinese science of acupuncture. The dragon's blood could then be identified with the energy running through the earth, through the goddess.

The symbology of the dragon provides a valuable cornerstone to understanding megalithic culture. The dragon represents the unleashed energies that activate sacred sites. These energies or ley lines, as previously mentioned, cover the earth in an intricate pattern. These lines were used for trade routes and for sacred sites. Ley lines are the paths of the dragon that humankind has yet to fully rediscover.

Megalithic people harnessed the dragon lines for particular magical purposes. They tapped into the dragon veins and the power that lay within. The conductors of the energy were the henges, earthworks, standing stones, dolmens, menhirs, and barrows—the subtle and involved alignments which are attuned to the nodal points of this energy. Audible sounds from energetic centers may actually be energetic noise from these power lines.

Originally called *Caerdemanon*, the standing stones at Stonehenge are considered to be a castle of the gods. The dragon power of this grouping of stones was raised by the priests for weather control, enhancing crop growth, healing, and communication. The dragon veins or ley lines connect the ancient sacred sites together into one massive generator of energy.

These dragon veins are represented by carvings on the stones, or by the positioning of standing stones. Numerous megalithic sites, like those at Callanish, Dorset, Avebury, and Stonehenge, have a twist or curve of stone avenues. This shows the serpent proceeding from the stone circle, representing the eternal procession of the son from the Mother. An affinity exists between the serpent-like concentric cup and channel markings and the nature of stars. Similar to the dragon veins, stars generate and transmit energy in spiral form. The cup markings could be representations of these dragon spiral-star energies.

Slaying the dragon was the practice of neutralizing or dispersing the energy generated by ancient sanctuaries. This energy was viewed as a live physical force, controlled and directed by a race of people whose knowledge became submerged in the collective mind.

This could explain why the dragon evolved into a negative symbol in certain cultures. Its energies could no longer be controlled, and they created havoc and destruction. Also figuring in this scenario is the glaring correlation between the Old Religion being replaced by Christianity. Serpents and dragons were associated with the earth goddess, only later identified as an aggressive male symbol embodying strength and force. People abandoned the womb-temple of the goddess for the thrusting phallic spire of her consort.

In America, Australia, and China, the mythological dragon and serpent represent the qualities of creative energy. In China, the dragon is a mysterious and vibrant sky and water symbol. The dragon symbolizes courage and nobility. In Europe the word "dragon" meant "chief," with the title "Pendragon" meaning "lord protector."

Rare sightings of dragons or dragon energy have occurred in the past. There are reports of people who've seen lions with wings that impart a feeling of divine love. Some have seen dragons as balls of bright fire with gold serpents intertwined together. These interlocking serpent shapes are interestingly similar to the spirals of the Celtic weave.

As a practitioner of magic, you are a sister or brother to dragons. The language of the dragon is one you can learn to understand. Many levels of reality exist, and are all part of a greater oneness. The magical world of dragons has its foundations in the energetic principles of polarity and flow. Are we waves or are we particles?

153

The dragon and the serpent are representative of the kundalini energy within each of us. Sexual expression and experience allow for the uncoiling of the symbolic serpent energy, awakening the power within. The dragons act as the ultimate creators of the unmanifested. They are magical tools of oneness, and they breathe out the fire of life. We are the dragons. The dragons are us. We are one. Travel with the goddess and her consort as they visit with the magical creatures, the dragon energy, on Samhain Eve.

Guided Journey: Samhain

The island is warm and private. The evening is still except for an occasional moist breeze sweeping from the ocean. She walks down the natural earth steps cut by the tides onto the sand. She waits for him on the beach, wearing a short violet robe made of lace and silk. She waits silently.

He comes to her in a small wooden boat gilded in golden light from the setting sun. She can hear the oars as they mate with the water and push the vessel toward the sandy shoreline. The rhythmic and compelling sound stirs the primal rhythms within her body.

She looks out over the water, at the tide as it moves in a similar rhythm, in and out. She begins to sway slightly back and forth to the motion as her mate moves his craft closer to its destination, to the eager woman awaiting him.

She turns her head slightly and notices the mist as it tumbles off the giant boulders in the distance, cast in the same golden light as her lover. The spray looks like a soft net of brilliance caressing the waves, dancing in and out, spiraling down and ricocheting back. Now and again the breeze carries the delicate mist on the wind, spreading it in an even greater pattern as it nestles into the sweeping tide.

Time shifts. A moment grows out of an eternity, as eternity grows out of a moment. At a time when the cold of winter should dwell, the warmth of the island sands permeates her body. She pushes her thighs and feet into the welcoming earth. The sand moves and gives way to the motion of her body.

The sound of the oars stops. The boat slides to shore, its hull decorated with large Theban designs. Her lover steps onto the wet sand and in one motion, he deftly secures his craft. He wears tight cobalt blue swim trunks that hug and accentuate every detail of his pelvis, thighs, and buttocks.

She rises out of the warm earth and walks toward him, their eyes locking in a magical embrace. He sees multi-colored spirals of light emanating from her wrists and ankles, shaped like beautiful mystical dragons. She weaves the dragon light in intricate patterns, knotting its threads about him, touching each part of his strong and hard body intimately, and electrifying the space between them.

They move to one another, holding hands gently. The spiraling energy from her wrists twists itself up along his arms, through his shoulders, sweeping across his chest, finally caressing his face in an odd magical glow.

Seagulls cry in the distance. Their faint calls grow louder, then fade again in the occasional breeze.

The man calls out loud to the earth, sea, and wind in an ancient tongue. His voice resonates through her body. The sound excites the dragons into flight, and together they are carried by the commanding tone.

Her arms turn to dragon wings. He can feel the wind pressing against his skin as she carries him to a secluded alcove down the shoreline. Her wings shimmer in the twilight as she sets them down upon the sand. They sit next to a bubbling spring flowing from a fissure in the sandstone that encircles the alcove.

She trails her hand, glowing with dragon light, through the cool water of the spring. The flowing water turns a soft green, then gold. She touches his cheek with her wet shining fingers before moving them into his thick hair. She kisses him slowly, softly at first, then deeply.

His hardening body responds to her caress. His breath quickens and pulse races. He holds her tighter and kisses her again, lifting her off the ground slightly.

Her body melds into his and the light from her limbs encases them in magical brilliance. To her, he smells of the sand, the forests, and water from the spring. To him, her scent is of flowers, thunderstorms, and the ocean.

The dragon light permeates them both, and the alcove becomes aglow. He moves the light as she does, directing the spirals over her shoulders, hair, and face.

She carefully weaves a delicate pattern of pearl-like light edged in blue and creates a magical harp made of sea shells for her lover to stroke and play upon.

He takes the harp. The light from his fingers sounds the strings before his hands touch the instrument. He plays her the Strain of Love, merging with the cadence and rhythm of the music.

The twilight turns to night, and the stars awaken to watch the lovers. He sets down the harp after a while, and it disappears with the tide. He fashions a beautiful tiara of gold and silver inlaid with pearls from the dragon light, and places it softly upon her head.

She transforms into pure light, warm, inviting, and wanting. She moves to him, gently rubbing her body against his. The intensity builds, and with it the dragon light grows and expands. Their arms transform into dragon wings, and they in turn become dragons of the night. Light spirals around them. As they join and move into one another, she feels as though she is flying.

As dragons, they ride together through the starry expanse in perfect rhythm. She can feel the movement of her wings. He can smell the sweat off his dragon hide.

His movements are slow, sensuous, and deliberate. She feels him fill her completely and matches his challenging pace. In the near distance, there is a blanket of light, mostly white, edged in gold. The dragon light pulls them toward the white light purposefully. The dragons know where they are going, ancient energy flowing back to the source.

The woman and man are the light. As dragons mating in flight, the lovers perform an ancient ritual, initiating the strongest bond. Together they fulfill the promise, bringing light to the world through their love and their oneness.

He emanates red dragon light, and she emanates green dragon light. Together they hurry toward the white light, a new threshold of reality beyond their imagination.

As she moves with him into the blanket of brilliance, a deeper desire takes hold of her body. Every sensation is intensified. Every movement of demanding maleness inside of her creates a deeper and more demanding need within her.

He flies her through the portal of white light. She cries out in pleasure as the first wave of her climax floods her senses. The dragon light shines more and more radiant, brighter and brighter. The light fills the woman. The spirals shooting from her body resemble a beautiful and powerful white dragon. The man fills with the same light. The spirals flying from his body mate with the white dragon, sliding in and out. They move into one another deeper, merging completely. Still higher they fly.

He is hot and flaming with dragon light. She responds totally to the light—giving, enticing, moaning his name in pleasure. Waves of delight wash wildly through her as they suddenly dive straight down into the sea. Her pulse quickens and her desire deepens. As dragons, the lovers frolic in the waves, pulling away from each other, then brushing against one another, hands trailing over skin. She beckons him to the shore, the same alcove, still softly aglow with dragon light. He carries her to a grassy spot against the sandstone and sets her on the ground, quickly moving into her, rhythmically and deliberately.

She is liquid, flowing like water. He is solid like the stones, and expansive like the sand. She flows into him like the tides moving into the sand. He grows more and more receptive to her. He feels damp with sweat. His strength gathers as he moves toward his release.

They spin and weave the dragon light until a ball of unearthly light becomes visible to the watching stars. Together they reach that sacred place of surrender and union. Together they cry out in the night, sending brilliant waves of delight sweeping across the sea and over the shoreline.

He spills into her. She receives him. Resting in the dragon light, the lovers turn and gaze quietly at one another. Her breathing matches his, gradually slowing. The spirals pulsing from his body match hers in uncanny unison. The dragon light bathes the lovers as the man softly sweeps the woman's hair away from her face and kisses her. They look up at the stars and smile.

❧

❧ A List of Goddesses and Consorts ❧

The following is a list of goddesses and consorts. There are four type of deities. First are the elven deities like Edain, Gobannon, and Mider. Second are the monadic deities including Rhiannon, Morrigan, and Triana. Third are the young gods, called the demi-gods. Cordemanon is in this group. The gods incarnate make up the fourth group of deities. These are goddesses and gods that have been born as humans, so that they may perform a specific task on earth.

Danu, Anu, Triana, and Morgana are aspects of the goddess Kerridwen. "Kerri" means "lady," and "dwen" means "white" or "bright." The Tuatha of Kerridwen and the Tuatha De Dannan are the same family. The Tuatha of Kerridwen refers to the members of the family who are presently human, incarnated on earth, while the Tuatha De Dannan describes the members of the family that are gods.

Danu or Anu was the mother monad of all gods. Bel or Belenus was the first monad to stem from Danu. The Dagda is the second monad, Bridget the third monad, and Llyr is the fourth monad to arise from Danu.

Amaethon: A god of agriculture and the harvest. Called the Harvest King. Appears with bronze, tanned skin, sun-streaked dark blond hair, blue or blue-green eyes, and a brilliant smile. He is a very friendly god. He wears green and brown tunics, or robes the color of wheat, corn, and grapes. His magical symbols are the fruits of the harvest and farmer's tools, particularly the sickle, hoe, and plow.

Andraste: Also Andrasta. A goddess of death, war, and fertility. Appears with dark skin, tall, and in green robes.

Angus: Also Angus Og, Oengus. A god of love and intimacy. Appears youthful with fair skin, red hair, and green eyes. His is full of fun, loving, and very well-endowed.

Arianrhod: A star and moon goddess similar to Sirona. A goddess of higher love and wisdom. Represents air of water. Appears very fair and gentle, her skin is translucent like starlight. She wears dark blue robes that are transparent or almost transparent. Her robes have a silver shimmer to them and are decorated with star-like jewels. "Arian" means "silver," and "rhod" means "wheel" or "disc." Her magical symbols are the crescent moon, stars, moonbeams, and a silver, eight-spoked wheel.

Artio: A bear goddess, the monad of all female bears. Appears large and strong. A protector of nature.

Balor: A sun god and king of the Formors.

Banba: A goddess representing Ireland.

Belenus: Also Bel, Belanos. A god of life, truth, inspiration, and music. Represents fire of fire. An active healing (dry heat) god. He drives away diseases. Appears as a radiant young man, with curly golden-blond hair and sky-blue eyes. He wears an unbelted robe of the whitest white, a sky blue robe, or goes nude. His magical symbols are the sun disc, a golden harp, a golden curved sword, and spear.

Belisama: A title of the goddess of fire, an aspect of Bridget but as the young sun, the sun maid. Her name means "like unto flame" or "bright and shining one." She wears transparent robes of sunrise colors and a white mantel and appears as fair, with bright sky-blue eyes and pale golden-blond hair. Her magical symbol is the rising sun.

Belisana: An aspect of Belisama with a similar appearance, but more earthy. Goddess of healing, laughter, and forests.

Boann: Also Boi, Boanna. A river goddess, and consort and wife of the Dagda. She is the mother of the herds. Her magical symbol is a silver salmon.

Bodb the Red: A son of the Dagda. He is virile and athletic and represents active male energy.

Borvo: Also Bormo, Bormanus. A Celtic Apollo, and a god of healing. Associated with wet heat, such as hot springs and mineral waters. Represents fire of water, and is a god of the unseen truth, and inspiration through dreams. Appears with golden skin, hair, and eyes, and wearing a golden tunic. His magical symbols are a flute, a golden harp, a golden sword or spear, hot springs, and the sun disc.

Bran: Also Bron. A protector of poets and bards. His features are similar to Gwydion. He is a handsome and manly god with long auburn hair and brown or green-brown eyes. Appears very tall, slender, and gentle. Appears with a beard and mustache most of the time. He wears blue, gold, yellow, and brown robes or nothing at all. His magical tool is the bard's harp and he is an excellent singer.

Branwen: A Welsh goddess of love, called the White-Bosomed One and the Venus of the Northern Sea. Her magical symbol is a white crow.

Bridget: A sun and fire goddess, fire of fire. She is the goddess of the hearth and home and represents the sacred fire. She is a goddess of smithcraft, healing, medicine, poetry, and inspiration. She is fair and bright, with sunny blue or green eyes, and honey-colored hair. She wears gold, brown, and golden-white robes or pastel shades of light blue and peach. Her magical symbols are the spindle and distaff, the sacred flame, a fire pot, and her brass shoe.

Brigantia: A powerful Celtic Briton nature goddess. Very similar to the sun goddess Bridget. An ancient name for Britain, representing rivers and the curves of the countryside.

Camulus: A Celtic Mars and war god, associated with clouds and storms. Appears with dark skin, brown eyes, and black hair. He wears a blood red tunic or dark charcoal-silver robes. His magical symbol is the severed head, and he carries a large sword.

Cliodna: A bird goddess and a young aspect of the Dark Goddess. Her name means "shapely one," and she is the most beautiful woman ever seen when she takes human form. Appears with black hair, brown eyes, and wears russet-colored robes. Her symbol is an apple.

Cordemanon: A young god of travel and knowledge. He appears as a handsome young man with golden hair and blue eyes. His magical symbols are stone circles and the Great Book of knowledge.

Coventina: A goddess of childbirth, renewal, and healing springs. Her well represents the womb of the earth. Appears with brown hair, brown eyes, and an earthy complexion. She wears brown robes the color of the earth. Her magical symbols are the womb and the well.

Dagda: Also The Dagda. He is an aspect of the All Father, and a lord of complete knowledge and wisdom. He is the Good God or the Good Hand, and is master of life and death and a bringer of prosperity and abundance. Twin to Sucellos as ruler of the bright half of the year. Appears with dark brown eyes and wavy brown hair. He is wise and very regal. Wears robes of cobalt blue and purple and sometimes peach or crimson-colored clothes. His magical tools are the rods of command, a chalice, a magic harp, the flesh hook, a sword, club, and cauldron.

Damona: A protectress of farmer's herds and fields and a goddess of abundance and prosperity. Her magical symbols are cattle.

165

Danu: Also Dana, Anna, Anu, Don. A goddess of wisdom, complete abundance, and control over all things; air of air. She is the greatest goddess, a goddess of the people. Appears as an old plump lady with gray hair, gray eyes, and gray robes. Sometimes she appears young and beautiful in bright green or white robes. Her magical symbols are a staff and the color green.

Diancecht: A physician of the gods. Appears with dark hair, brown eyes, and with a fair or ruddy complexion. He wears blue or silver robes, and his magical tools are the mortar and pestle.

Dumiatis: Also Dumeatis. A master teacher god of creative thought, a Celtic Mercury. Similar to the god Lugh. Appears tall and slender with a brilliant smile, and dark curly brown hair and golden eyes. He has a quiet intensity and is often seen sitting on a hill or under a tree surrounded by children who are listening to his teachings. His magical symbols are the quill pen and ink, writing staves, books of knowledge, and the teaching tales.

Dwyn: A god of love and mischief who loves to play tricks. Appears youthful with dark skin, hair, and eyes. He is noted as being extremely manly and very well-endowed.

Edain: Also Etain. A goddess of grace and beauty and wife of Mider, who won her in a chess game. An example of transmigration. Appears fair, with golden hair, blue eyes, and wearing blue and gold robes tied with a golden belt. Her magical symbols are a herd of white mares with blue eyes and a spray of apple blossoms held in her hand.

Elayne: Also Elen, Elen Lwyddawg. She is the Leader of the Hosts, and considered the Warrior Mother; also called Eriu, goddess of Ireland. A goddess of war and leadership and of immense stature. Myrddin is one of her consorts.

Epona: An earth goddess representing fertilization by water, and a horse goddess. Appears as fair-skinned with black hair and gray eyes. She wears blue and gray robes and is portrayed holding an apple while seated on a horse.

Esus: A woodland god and aspect of the dark face of Kernunnos. He is a woodsman and hunter who slays Tarvos, the golden bull. Appears tall, strong, and muscular. Wears animal skins and carries a sword and bow.

Fagus: A tree god representing the monad of all beeches.

Fliodhas: A goddess of the woodlands and woodland animals, associated with the deer goddess Sadv. She protects animals and the woodlands. She calls the wild animals of the woodlands her cattle. Appears as a quiet and shy goddess, with long wavy honey-colored hair. She wears brown tunics and breeches, but is also seen in robes of woodland greens and crowned with ferns and flowers. She has a sunny personality. Her magical symbols are a large doe, lush green grass, and woodland springs.

Gabba: A goddess of the Abyss, a crone aspect of the Dark All Mother, and one of the dark queens. No one knows or remembers what she looks like. Her symbol is the Celtic endless weave.

Gobannon: Also Govannon, Goibniu. A blacksmith god of magic. Works with metals and forges. Appears dark complected, with dark brown eyes and black hair. Wears a brown tunic with a leather apron. His magical symbols are blacksmithing tools and the transforming fire.

Gwalchmei: Called the Hawk or Falcon of May, as the son of the goddess Mei. He portrays a god of love and music. His symbols are raptors and the fields at hunting times, in the early morning and late afternoon.

Gwydion: Is the son of Don (Danu). He is a god of kindness, the arts, eloquence and magic; a master of illusion and fantasy, and helper of humankind. He is the brother of Amaethon and Gobannon. He is brother and consort to Arianrhod. Gwydion has two sons, Dylan and Lleu (Lugh). Math, son of Mathonwy, handed on his knowledge and abilities (which are infinite) to his student and nephew, Gwydion. Gwydion is bard and wizard, prince of the powers of the air, a shape-shifter. Appears as fair with short blondish-brown hair and blue eyes. Wears a blue or gray robe or tunic. He is a great enchanter and healer, and his magical symbol is a harp.

Gwyn ap Nudd: Also Gwyn. A god of the Wild Hunt. A god of the death chase and god of the Otherworld. He is the hunter of souls and lord of the unmanifested. Appears as very fair, almost white, with icy blue eyes. He has a very large body and moves with great strength. His magical symbol is a white hound with red ears named Dormarth.

Hellith: A god of the setting sun (fire of air), and of the dying. If invoked, he brings peace to those near death. After death, souls are in his protection until they reach their destination. He is a gentle young man with pale blond hair and very fair skin. Wears white robes with a violet hue. Also appears with hair, eyes, skin and robe of one color, the color of the red embers of a dying fire. His magical symbols are the setting sun disc and a flute that brings peace and tranquility to those who hear it.

Hertha: Also Herdda. A goddess of rebirth and healing. She is an earth goddess, representing the greening of spring. Appears with brownish hair, green or brown eyes, and is very well-endowed. She wears brown and green robes. Her magical symbols are the cow, calf, and milk pail.

Kernunnos: The All Father, and a god of wealth. He is lord of the animals, and a god of life and death. Appears with medium long, curly brown hair, fair and ruddy skin, and brown or hazel eyes. He wears a short tunic. His magical symbols are animal horns, a serpent belt, a stag, a bull, three cranes, a rat, and a bag of flowing coins.

Kerridwen: The All Mother. A goddess of inspiration and knowledge, called The Ninefold One. Looks translucent like moonlight, sometimes like a white fog or a brilliant point of light. She wears robes of white and her face is bright, and pure light radiates from her eyes. Her magical symbol is a large cauldron from which all manifested energy arises.

Letha: A harvest goddess associated with Midsummer. Appears with honey-brown hair and hazel eyes, wearing robes of silver and gray, or golden-brown. Her magical symbols are a swan and apples.

Llyr: Also Ler, Lir. A god of the sea and a king of the oceans. He is a shy god who rarely reveals himself, and can appear as a part-man, part-fish creature. He is very gentle and loving, but if provoked can turn to rage. Appears kingly and very handsome. His skin is faintly green and seems to sparkle like moonlight shining on the ocean, almost translucent. He has silver-white hair, a beard and mustache, and pale green-blue eyes the color of the ocean. He wears gray and sea-foam green robes or goes nude. His magical symbols are sea shells, sharks, sea mammals, the sea serpent, and seagulls. He plays a harp that he fashioned with silver, pearl, coral, and shell.

Luchta: Also Lucta, Luchtaine. A god of smiths, wrights, and craftsmen. Associated with Gobannon. He is the Carpenter God, and the shield maker for the Tuatha. Appears with blue eyes, blond-brown hair, and wears a belted tunic in brown or gold. His magical symbol is the shield.

Lugh: Also Lug, Lleu, Llew. Uncontested master of all arts. A god of war, smiths, poets, and bards, associated with the setting sun and the moon. He is a champion of the Tuatha, a historian and powerful sorcerer. Appears very handsome and clean shaven, with dark brown hair and blue eyes. Very lusty appetite and known for his generosity and prowess. His magical symbols are the cock, turtle, goat, a magic sword, and a bag of coins.

Manannan: Also Manannan Ap Llyr, Manannan Mac Llyr. A god of the sea and travel, and a magician. He is a master shape-shifter and great teacher. Appears tall, dark, and handsome. He wears black or dark charcoal robes, sometimes belted in a gold chain. His magical symbols are a wand, a magic coracle, a magic spear called Red Javelin, and several magic swords, three of which are called The Great Fury, The Little Fury, and Retaliator.

Math: A Welsh god of sorcery, magic, and enchantment. He is a master druid, teacher, and king. Math is the seasonal king, and is symbolic of the cycle of life, death, and rebirth. Math is king of the empire and has great wealth and knowledge. Uncle and teacher to Gwydion, he is protective, powerful, and wise. Nothing escapes his attention. He is older, but virile and handsome. He has white in his hair, the bluest of eyes, and wears light blue or white robes. His magical symbol is the fabric of life.

Medb: Also Maeve, Mab. A goddess of the land's sovereignty, she is the good queen, called The Warrior Queen. She is the Faery Queen and Queen of Connaught. Appears with flame-red hair, green eyes, and wears orange-red robes. She is magnificent and powerful, runs faster than horses, and carries animals and birds on her arms and shoulders. Her magical tools are the spear and shield.

Mei: Also Mai, Meia. An earth and sun goddess, similar to Rosemerta. She is the mother of Gwalchmei. She has long dark golden-brown hair, blue eyes, and wears sky-blue or meadow-green robes.

Mider: A Gaelic god of the Otherworld, called the Faery King. A bard and chess player, he likes to play games for high stakes. He is a Celtic Pluto and consort to Etain.

Modrona: Also Motrona. A goddess associated with Coventina and an aspect of the All Mother.

Morgana: A goddess of war, fertility, and magic. She is the Death Mother or the Queen of Death. She is the daughter of Llyr and Anu. Appears as fair or ruddy, with long black, blue-black or reddish-black hair, and dark brown, green, or blue-black eyes. She has awesome beauty and is very sensuous. Appears as a young woman or can look like an ugly hag. She wears wine-red, indigo, or black robes. Her magical symbols are trees along the shoreline, sea shells, cypress tress, ravens, and crows.

Morrigan: Also Morrigana. She is called the Sea Queen and the Great Sea Mother. She is a goddess of wisdom and appears very queenly. She is a statuesque woman, with long dark silver-streaked hair, opalescent skin, and gray-green eyes. She wears deep sea green and blue robes, tied with a cord of white or shell pink. She wears a tiara of gold, silver, and pearl. Her magical symbols are the queen's rod of command, sand dollars, ocean vegetation, manta rays, and whales.

Morrigu: A goddess of death, life, and magic. She is called the Dark Gray Lady or the Queen of the Sea. She protects sailors and the shores of Erin. Appears with dark indigo eyes, dark silver-gray hair, and opalescent skin. She has a gentle nature but if angered, she destroys. She wears pale green robes, or sometimes gray-green, silver, or dark blue robes. Her magical symbols are a harp of silver, shell and pearl, and ocean caves.

Myrddin: A sun and earth god, fire of earth. A god of woodlands and nature, laughter and mirth. A sky-god associated with stones, caves, crystals, woodlands, and magic. A god of healing associated with herbs, natural mineral deposits, and pure water springs. Appears as a younger robust man, with reddish brown hair and hazel green eyes. He wears short brown or forest green belted tunics, and has woodland flowers tangled in his curly hair, beard, and mustache. His magical symbols are the wild rose, sweet water springs, and he plays a flute whose sound urges you to laugh and dance.

Nantosuelta: A goddess of abundance who is associated with Sucellos. She is a river goddess. Appears as fair and rosy with brown hair and brown eyes. She wears blue-green robes, and holds a dove house on a pole in one hand, and sometimes carries a baker's paddle.

Nemetona: A goddess of the oak grove, and a warrior goddess, who is the great protectress of the sacred Drynemeton and a patron of thermal springs. She is gentle and friendly, with dark skin, long dark hair, and dark eyes. She wears a short brown warrior's tunic and sandals or brown belted robes. Her magical symbols are oak groves, a ram, and a spear made of ash wood with a silver tip.

Nimue: An earth and water goddess, and a young aspect of the Bright All Mother. She is goddess of lakes, also known as the Lady of the Lake, maker and keeper of Excalibur, King Arthur's sword. She is a student and teacher of Myrddin, her consort. She has knee-length dark brown hair, large blue-green or blue-violet eyes, fair skin, and large man-like hands. She wears robes of soft blues, lavenders, whites and aquas, or goes nude. Her magical symbols are a large, bright white-silver sword, underwater caves, swans, swallows, and quartz and crystalline formations.

Nodens: A god of sleep and dreams, dream magic, and a god of the Otherworld. He has light hair and eyes and wears light colored robes.

Nuada: Also Lludd, Nudd. A Celtic Jupiter and an aspect of the All Father, the Good Father. He is a god of wealth, war, kingship, and thunder. Appears as fair, with silver-gray eyes, and grayish-white hair and beard. He wears a very short brown or dark charcoal-colored tunic, and is good natured with a great appetite. He has a silver arm made by Diancecht. His magical symbols are a magic spear, thunder, and lightning.

Nwyvre: A god of the ethers and space, also god of celestial sciences, astronomy, and astrology. He is a god of space and stars and is consort to Arianrhod. Appears as fair, almost translucent like starlight, very gentle, and wears robes of dark blues or silver. His magical symbol is the nine-pointed star.

Ogmios: Also Ogma. A god of civilization and the inventor of writing (Oghams). Appears as fair with brilliant blue eyes, and light brown or silver-brown hair. He is lusty, well-endowed, handsome, and very knowledgeable. He wears a blue or brown tunic, belted with silver. His magical symbols are a club or stick with runes carved on it.

Pryderi: A master of disguise and shape-shifter. He brought the swine from the Otherworld. He is the son of Rhiannon. Appears in many shapes, usually young and athletic. His magical symbol is the pig or boar.

Pwyll: A ruler of the Otherworld, and Prince of Dyfed. He is always seen with a pack of hounds.

Rhiannon: A goddess of knowledge, and an aspect of the All Mother. She is called Queen Mother and is associated with horses as the Queen Mare. She was originally called

Rigatona or the Great Queen. Appears as fair and bright with reddish-brown hair and green or blue eyes. She wears robes of bright reds or red-browns, or silver and gray. Her magical symbols are apples, a mare, and three birds.

Robur: A god of forests, in particular oaks, the monad of all oaks. He is a tree god known as the Forest King. Sometimes he appears with bright gray eyes, a wild unruly white beard, and silvery white hair and mustache. His skin is the color of tree bark and he goes nude or dressed in a leather tunic. He often has mistletoe tangled in his hair and beard. His magical symbols are mistletoe, a budding staff of oak, and woodland animals.

Rosemerta: A goddess of abundance and plenty. Lugh is her consort and she is a young aspect of the All Mother. She has a rosy complexion, with honey-colored or auburn hair, and green-brown eyes. She wears robes colored with warm hues of red, brown, and green. Her magical symbols are gardens and a cornucopia flowing out with all good things.

175

Sadv: A goddess of the forests. She is called the Deer Goddess. Mother to Oisin, the poet. Appears with white hair, dark blue-gray eyes, and wears scarlet robes tied with a silver belt. Her magical symbols are the doe with a fawn, and other woodland animals.

Sirona: A Celtic Venus and goddess of the sun and the stars. Her consort is Borvo. She is fair with dark reddish-brown or black hair, and deep green or indigo eyes. She has a star on her forehead and wears dark blue or silver robes with star-like jewels. Her magical symbol is the star.

Smertullos: A god of the abyss and associated with the unmanifested. He is called the Preserver and Lord of Protection. He appears with red hair, fair skin, and blue eyes, and wears brown and white robes. His magical symbols are a snake with a ram's head and a snake belt.

Sucellos: A god of death and fertility, an aspect of the All Father. He is the Dagda's twin as ruler of the dark half of the year. He has such beauty that to look upon his face would bring death, so he appears in many disguises and shapes; sometimes he appears odd and humorous. His magical tool is a large spear.

Taranis: A god of the passing seasons, storms, and thunder. He is very fair-skinned with blue eyes. He has long wild hair and a beard. He wears a white tunic and mantle, and his magical symbol is the eight-spoked wheel.

Tarvos Trigaranos: A god of vegetation and a young aspect of Kernunnos. Born at Coventina's well, he is built like a bull and his form is perfect. He is virile and athletic. His hair is light brown and his eyes are very intense, usually blue or brown. His magical symbols are oaks and three gray cranes.

Tethra: A shadowy god of the sea and magic; air of water. Appears with golden-brown curly hair, green eyes, and wears gray-green robes. He has the appearance of moonbeams on the ocean. His magical symbols are the albatross and a flock of seagulls.

Ti Ana: Also Ty Ana, De Ana, Dy Ana. A goddess of the house and home. Her name means "Thy Mother" or "Ana of the Household."

Triana: The Threefold Mother. She portrays three faces of the goddess. Sun-Ana is a goddess of healing, knowledge, and mental arts. She wears a white robe with a bright yellow mantle, which is clasped together at the breast with a golden sun disc. Earth-Ana is a goddess of nature, life, and death. She wears a green robe with a brown mantle which is clasped together with a copper broach inlaid with three green leaves. Moon-Ana is a goddess of higher love and wisdom. She wears a gray robe with a blue mantle which is clasped together with a silver crescent moon.

Viviana: Also Vivian. A goddess of birth and life, and an aspect of the All Mother. She is a bright goddess of life and love, of mothers and childbirth, and of children. Her name means "Life Mother." She has golden streaks in her hair and green or blue eyes. She wears a golden-white or spring green robe. Her magical symbol is the five-petaled red rose.

ঞ Goddess Color Correspondence Table ৶

Colors reflect light, and are effective symbols in magic. Gwydonnic tradition incorporates the effectiveness of color in its teachings. Suggested uses for color and the corresponding goddesses serve as references for the practitioner.

Red
Corresponds to passion, sex, the physical body, dynamic force, vitality, virility, blood, healing, rebirth, power, animation, and emotional desire. Brigantia, Rhiannon, Morgana, Medb, Viviana, and Elayne typify the color red.

Orange
Corresponds to pleasure, joy, feeling good, being open, generosity, happiness, gladness, mirth, ease and comfort, prosperity and plenty. The color orange represents the hearth and home and the origination of patterns and ritual. Bridget, Rosemerta, Hertha, and Belisama typify this color.

Yellow and Gold
Correspond to orange, and add a youthful emphasis. Gold relates to knowledge, learning, teaching, studying, understanding, cognition, truth, fact, lore, comprehension, and perception. Belisana, Ty Ana, Viviana, Nimue, and Bridget typify the colors of yellow and gold.

Brown
Corresponds to the earth, soil, potential, nurturing, and rebirth. Hertha, Cliodna, Coventina, Epona, Fliodhas, Modrona, and Nemetona typify the color brown.

Green

Corresponds to creating positive physical patterns, birth, spring greening, healing, the home, prosperity, abundance, regeneration and renewal, growth, the young and the tender in nature. Danu, Rosemerta, Hertha, Viviana, Fliodhas, Sadv, Belisana, Ty Ana, Damona, Mei, Artio, and Andraste all typify the color green.

Blue

Corresponds to divination, dreams, intuition, loyalty, defensive protection, cleansing, water, creative arts, dance, and emotions. Arianrhod, Morrigan, Nimue, Boann, Sirona, Mei, Edain, Nantosuelta, and Morrigu typify the color blue.

Violet

Corresponds to lore, ancestral intuition, sacredness, consecration, offensive protection, pattern making and breaking, ancestral memory, and healing through destroying disease. Danu, Nimue, Sirona, Morrigan, Elayne, and Morgana typify the color violet.

White

Corresponds to the manifested, divine energy, ritual, positivity, perfection, pureness, and love. Kerridwen, Branwen, Nimue, and Bridget typify the color white.

Gray

Corresponds to wisdom, oneness, merging, cosmic consciousness, creative life force, and feeling centered. Rhiannon, Morrigan, Sirona, Edain, Morrigu, Arianrhod, Epona, Gabba, and Letha all typify the color gray.

Rose

Corresponds to higher love, enlightenment, nirvana, godhood. Danu, Nimue, Branwen, and Rosemerta typify the color rose.

◈ Feather Augury Chart ◈

Most of us have happened upon bird feathers while out walking in nature. Gwyddonic tradition includes the ancient custom of gathering feathers and using them as symbolic communication tools. You can use feathers to send a secret message to your lover or friend. Combining feathers of different colors can say a great deal to those who make an effort to understand the meanings of feather augury.

Feather Color	Symbolic Meanings
White	Pureness, gladness, a birth
Green	New prospects, adventure, money
Red	Fortune and good luck
Rose	A love affair, romance
Blue	Love, a gift
Brown	Good health
Yellow	Friendship, companionship
Orange	Happiness to come in the future
Gray	Peace of mind, tranquility
Purple	A journey or trip
Blue and White	A new love
Brown and White	Health and happiness
Gray and White	A new and positive situation
Black and White	Beware, be cautious
Black	Misfortune, bad luck, death, the unknown
Yellow and Green	Gossip and small talk

❧ Stones and Suggested Uses ☙

Stone	Suggested Uses and Qualities
Agate	Emotional and physical balancing, digestion, grounding
Amethyst	Spiritual development, courage, psychic growth
Aquamarine	Clarity of mind, flow, inspiration
Adventurine	Positive participation, active imagination, travel
Azurite	Amplifies healing ability, mental clarity
Bloodstone	Creativity, vitality, circulation of energy, higher knowledge
Carnelian	Sexuality, fire energy, power, and creativity
Citrine	Thinking process, mental clarity, patterning, insight
Clear Quartz	Healing, balancing energy, sight and clarity, spirituality
Calcite	Balancing positive and negative energies within the body
Diamond	Strength, power, insight, inspiration, protection, development

Emerald	Psychic clarity, divination, growth, patterning, sexuality
Fluorite	Otherworld experience, projecting a sense of peace
Garnet	Strength in physical body, love and passion, imagination, flow
Hematite	Grounding, protection, strength, density, the shadow self
Herkimer	Dreaming, higher love, stimulating psychic centers, power
Jade	Protection, divine love, connection with earth, cleansing
Lapis Lazuli	Psychic development, divination, protection, creativity, power
Malachite	Communication with nature, rapport with animal kingdom, balance
Moonstone	Connection to female energy, receptivity, tidal flow, emotions
Opal	Harmony, cosmic energy, creativity and wisdom, balance
Pyrite	Prosperity, circulation and flow, generating energy
Rose Quartz	Emotional balancing, relationships and friendships, higher love
Ruby	Power, insight, creativity, physical and mental strength, drive

Rutile	Building energy, balance, insight, health, patterning
Sapphire	Psychic development, creativity, passion, stimulates energy
Smoky Quartz	Grounding, centering, earth connection, healing, prosperity
Topaz	Insight, knowledge, loyalty, higher love, creativity
Tourmaline	Strengthens energy body, regeneration, creativity, growth

❧ Chart to Calculate Great Days and Moons ❧

Begin with the first Full Moon after Yule.

1. Wolf
2. Storm
3. Chaste
4. Seed
5. Hare
6. Dyad
7. Mead
8. Wort
9. Barley
10. Wine
11. Blood
12. Snow
13. Oak

Earth
North-Yule
First Great Day

Samhain

Bridget's Fire

Water
West
Hellith's Day

Air
East
Lady's Day

Lughnassad

Beltane

Fire
South
Letha's Day

187

Note: Oak is not used in 12-Moon years.

Path of the Sun — from Yule Clockwise to Samhain

- Yule, Winter Solstice at 00.00 degrees Capricorn
- Bridget's Fire at 15.00 degrees Aquarius
- Hertha's Day, Spring Equinox at 00.00 degrees Aries
- Beltane at 15.00 degrees Taurus
- Letha's Day, Summer Solstice at 00.00 degrees Cancer
- Lughnassad at 15.00 degrees Leo
- Hellith's Day, Autumnal Equinox at 00.00 degrees Libra
- Samhain at 15.00 degrees Scorpio

৯ Alphabets ৯

The Oghams

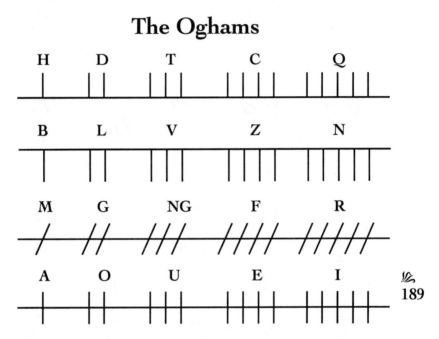

There are three forms of covert sign language used by the Ancients. They are Hand Ogham, Nose Ogham, and Shin Ogham. All three had certain concepts in common.

Nose Ogham: Uses the nose as a baseline and the five fingers (four plus thumb) to form the letters on the nose in four groups.

Shin Ogham: Uses the shin bone to represent the whale's back or baseline. Form the individual letters in the same way as they are in the Nose Oghham.

Hand Ogham: Indicates each of the 20 letters by a particular finger joint, pointing to one, or displaying one. Also you can make the letters with fingers themselves.

The Theban Alphabet

A	B	C	D	E

F	G	H	I	J

K	L	M	N	O

P	Q	R	S	T

U	V	W	X	Y

Z

Futharken Runes

The Futhark rune system has three major functions: as an alphabet, for divination, and for magic.

A   OS (god)
B   beorc (birch)
D   daeg (day)
E   eoh (horse)
F   feh (money)
G   geofu (gift)
H   heagl (hail)
I   is (ice)
J   gear (year)
K   can (torch)
L   lagu (water, sea)
M   man (human being)
N   nied (need)
O   eoel (inheritance, noble)
P   peod (dance)
R   eolhs (stones)
S   sygil (sun)
T   tir (honour, war)
U   ur (aurocks, ox)
W   wynn (joy)
TH   thorn (thorn)
NG   ing (a hero)

Futharken Alphabet

≫ Glossary ≪

All Father: The consort.

All Mother: The goddess.

Amulet: An object, traditionally metal or stone, that has two or more feelings or effects placed in it.

Archetypes: Symbolic representations of universal principles. Defining concepts in a symbolic form.

Art and Craft: The ancient goddess tradition, or Old Religion.

Athame: A ceremonial knife, two-sided and flame-like. A ceremonial tool representing the element fire.

Aura: Body of light surrounding the human body. Traditionally egg-shaped or upside-down egg-shaped; however, they change with individuals and emotions.

Avalon: Land of the Otherworld, where the gods live.

Bard: Class of priest—poet and harpist. Wrote and sang about historical and legendary events.

Belenus: A solar diety. In Scottish, it means May Day.

Beltane: Great Day at the beginning of May. Also known as Bel Fire. "Bel" means "bright."

Boon Moon: A High Moon, the sixth full moon after Yule.

Boundless: A vast and infinite place of being. Oneness.

Bridget's Fire: The second Great Day, following Yule.

Bright One: The Bright aspects of the All Mother representing light and life.

Celtic: The ancient Gauls and Britons. Welsh, Irish, Highland Scot, Manx, Cornish, and Breton people of central and western Europe described as being fair and tall.

Centering: An exercise or point of development in which one's mind is constantly turned toward the concept of oneness, where one is continually aware of the boundless.

Chalice: A loving cup traditionally made of metal or clay. A consecrated tool symbolizing the water element and the concept of oneness.

Conditioning: State of being that reflects the culmination of one's ancestry, upbringing, experience, personality, and culture. Not the true self, but a collection of valences and reactions that an individual wears as a way to maneuver in the world.

Coracle: A small boat covered with animal skins.

Cordemanon: Family of the Southern Queen. The name of a young god, and the ancient name for Stonehenge. Also means an individual who teaches the Gwyddonic tradition without distortion.

Dark One: The Dark aspect of the All Mother who represents death.

Days of Power: The eight Great Days of ritual celebration.

Divination: The art and science of forecasting or reading events using traditional tools, such as runes or tarot cards.

Double: A duplicate self that arises out of one's primary self.

Doubling Out: The process of creating a double.

Dragon: Symbol of unmanifested energy.

Dragon Light: The visible energy that is generated by the dragon lines or veins.

Dragon Lines or Veins: Channels of energy that run through the earth, our bodies, and the cosmos.

Dreaming: A state of consciousness.

Ego: One's individual awareness system.

Eight-Spoked Wheel: The wheel of the sun which includes the eight Great Days. Each spoke denotes one of these days.

Elemental: A non-biological form. Traditionally living in stone or metal, or any object. An awareness or mind without a body. See Pooka.

Elements: Four traditional elements: earth, air, fire, water. The fifth element is the practitioner.

Equinoxes: Solar cycles between the solstices.

Fabric of Life: The endless Celtic weave representing the totality of all manifest reality.

Feast: A celebration meal in honor of the goddess and her consort.

Female Energy: The goddess, represented by the color green, and associated with the left side and the state of being receptive.

Four Wards: The four corners of North, East, South, and West. Also called the Watch Towers or the Great Wards.

Full Moons: The 12-13 full moons of the yearly cycle, beginning with the first full moon after Yule. Each moon has its own qualities. A time of healing rituals.

God: An individual male being who lives in a merged state.

Goddess: An individual female being who lives in a merged state.

Godhood: The attainment of becoming a God. A being who has gone through the three great merges, and moves beyond time and space.

Granting of the Boon: A request of a gift from the goddess. A boon is a blessing and a gift.

Great Adventure: Birth, life, death, and rebirth.

Great Book: Also known as the Book of Shadows. A traditional book teaching the Art and Craft, and copied by hand by a student. Made available to those who are initiated.

Great Circle: A protective circle of light constructed by the practitioner for magical works.

Great Days: The eight Great Days, the Wheel of Taranos, including the solstices, the equinoxes, and the midpoints.

Gwyddon: Magician, Wise One, Astrologer, or Healer.

Gwyddonic Druidic tradition: A spiritual and philosophical way to improve one's life process based on the concept of oneness.

Handfasting: Traditional wedding ritual. Culminates in the Great Rite, the sacred union between a woman and man.

Harp: A stringed musical instrument. The number of strings on a harp has special meaning. A bard's magical tool (Telyn).

Hellith's Day: The seventh Great Day, usually celebrating the harvest which takes place on the Autumnal Equinox.

High Magic: Magical works done on the Great Days and on the High Moons while in rapport with the goddess and her consort.

High Priest: Traditionally a third degree male who administers the desires of the High Priestess. The arm of the law. Represents the god or consort in ritual.

High Priestess: A third degree female. The avenue of the Goddess, and represents the Goddess in form and in ritual.

Individuality: The essence portion of a human being that lives from life to life. The eternal part of one's being.

Initiation: Being initiated into the Art and Craft. The birth of one's true self.

Invocation: A magical technique for calling an entity.

Lady's Day: Also called Hertha's Day. The third Great Day of the cycle, associated with the beginning of spring. Held on the eve of the spring equinox.

Leisure: Activity one engages in based on individual choice and perceived personal freedom. Generally a pleasant activity.

Letha's Day: The fifth Great Day of the cycle. Also called Midsummer.

Ley Lines: Currents of energy that run through the earth in a grid-like system. The energy can be tapped and used. Sacred sites, churches, trade routes, and wells are located along ley lines. See Dragon Lines.

Lughnassad: The sixth Great Day; it takes place in August. Lugh's wedding feast. Considered the time when the forces of light and dark converge, when the sun and moon are equal.

Mabinogen: Bardic tales and stories of the lives of heroines and heros.

Magic: The study of nature and the use of ritual to continue the cycle of the goddess and her consort.

Magic Mirror: A magical tool used for seeing, while in a merged state.

Magical Arts: Creating matter and energy out of the unmanifested or the manifested. Patterning one's life by using the Art and Craft.

Magical Tools: Items representing the elements that have been consecrated by a High Priestess and High Priest or by the goddess and her consort.

Magician: One who practices magic, a practitioner.

Male Energy: The consort, represented by the color red and associated with the right side and the state of emitting.

Manifested: Tangible reality.

Matriarchal: Based on the goddess as head of the family or Tuatha. Descent, kinship, and succession are determined through the mother.

Merging: The state of becoming one with all things. Diffusing into the boundless.

Negativity: An energetic force that breaks patterns and feeds upon itself. Associated with the Dark One.

Oghams: Form of writing invented by the consort Ogmios.

Old Religion: The goddess tradition.

Oneness: The boundless. A place where one is connected to all things and nothing.

Patterns: A term for discussing one's expectations and intentions. The method or foundation from which one merges.

Pentagram: A five-pointed star.

Pooka: A companion and elemental being. Helpful and beneficial.

Portal: A door to another world or reality.

Positivity: An energetic force which creates pattern. Associated with the Bright One.

Practitioner: A person who practices magic.

Prana: The vital force of essence.

Prophecy: To predict under divine influence and direction.

Rapport: Harmony of relationship with another, to be in close accord. Remembering who we really are, and understanding the deeper connection.

Rune: Letters with magical qualities. Secret letters, secret knowledge, secret powers, magical symbols.

Running the Light: Moving mass amounts of energy during a magical work or with a sexual partner during lovemaking.

Salt: Represents the earth element. Used for purifying and clearing energy.

Samhain: All Hallows Eve and the eighth Great Day, associated with death and rebirth. The day when the veil between time and space is the thinnest.

Seeker: A person interested in the Art and Craft. The name of an initiate.

Solstice: Time during summer and winter when the sun is at its greatest distance from the celestial equator. A day of power.

Sunwise: Clockwise turn which is considered the positive direction. The opposite of widdershins or moonwise.

Symbols: Representation of many things in one thing.

Synchronicity: When two things occur at exactly the same time. Having the same vibrational energy. To time things together for a particular outcome.

Tarot Cards: A divination tool.

Theban: Ancient form of writing.

Three Eyes of Kerridwen: The formula for magical works—expectation, desire, and merging.

Threefold One: The Triple Goddess representing birth, life, and death.

Tir-nan-Og: Land of Promise, the Celtic paradise.

Tuatha: The family.

Tuatha of Kerridwen: The family of Kerridwen, goddesses and gods in human incarnate form.

Tuatha De Dannan: The family of Danu, name of the gods.

Unmanifested: Non-tangible reality. That which does not exist as yet, energy that has not been born.

Wand: Traditionally of wood, represents the element air.

White Goddess: Considered to be Kerridwen, the Bright One.

Widdershins: Counterclockwise movement. Associated with negativity. Moonwise.

Wizard: A sorcerer and wise person.

Yule: The first Great Day, celebrated on the winter solstice.

❧ Bibliography ❧

Alder, Margot. *Drawing Down the Moon*. Boston, MA: Beacon Press, 1981.

Araoz, Daniel L. *The New Hypnosis*. New York, NY: Brunner-Mazel Publishers, 1985.

Bandler, Richard, and John Grinder. *Patterns of Hypnotic Techniques of Milton H. Erickkson, Vol. 1*. New York, NY: Brunner-Mazel Publishers, 1979.

——*The Structure of Magic*. Palo Alto, CA: Science and Behavior Books, 1975.

Bonwick, James. *Irish Druids and Old Irish Religions*. New York, NY: Dorset, 1986.

Bord, Janet and Colin Bord. *Mysterious Britain*. London, England: Paladin Books, 1974.

——*The Secret Country*. New York, NY: Walker and Co., 1977.

Bricklin, Mark. *Positive Living and Health*. Emmaus: Rodale Press, Inc., 1990.

Briggs, Katherine. *An Enclyclopedia of Fairies*. New York, NY: Pantheon Books, 1976.

Bry, Adelaide. *Directing the Movies of Your Mind*. New York, NY: Harper and Row Publishers, 1978.

Campbell, Joseph. *A Hero With a Thousand Faces*. Bollinger Series. Princeton, NJ: Princeton University Press, 1973.

—— *The Masks of God*, Vol I—IV. New York, NY: Penguin Books, 1977.

Ceram, C. W. *Gods, Graves and Scholars.* New York, NY: Bantam Books, 1972.

Chopra, Deepak, M.D. *Unconditional Life: Mastering the Forces that Shape Personal Reality.* New York, NY: Bantam Books, 1991.

Conway, D. J. *Celtic Magic.* St. Paul, MN: Llewellyn Publications, 1990.

Cunningham, Scott. *Living Wicca.* St. Paul, MN: Llewellyn Publications, 1993.

De Troyes, Chretian. *Arthurian Romances.* New York, NY: Dutton, 1967.

Denning, Melita, and Phillips Osbourne. *Mysterica Magica, Book V.* St. Paul, MN: Llewellyn Publications, 1981.

Edmonston, William E. (Jr.). *Hypnosis and Relaxation: Modern Verification of An Old Equation.* New York, NY: John Wiley and Sons, 1981.

Eliade, Micea. *Shamanism.* Bollingen Series. Princeton, NJ: 1964.

Frazier, Sir James George. *The Golden Bough.* New York, NY: The Macmillan Company, 1935.

Gantz, Jeffrey, translator. *The Mabinogion.* Middlesex, England: Dorset Press, 1976.

Gawain, Shakti. *Creative Visualization.* Mill Valley, CA: Whatever Publishing, 1978.

Graves, Robert. *The White Goddess.* New York, NY: Faber & Faber, 1966.

Gruffydd, W. J. *Folklore and Myth in the Mabinogion,* Cardiff, Wales: University of Wales Press, 1975.

Howard, Michael. *The Magic of Runes.* New York, NY: Samuel Weiser, 1980.

Hutchison, Michael. *Megabrain.* New York, NY: Random House, 1986.

Jacobs, Joseph, collected by. *Celtic Fairytales.* New York, NY: Dover Publications, Inc., 1968.

Kazin, Alfred, selected and arranged by. *The Portable Blake*. New York, NY: The Viking Press, 1946.

Krishnamurti, J. *The Flight of the Eagle*. New York, NY: Harper and Row Publishers, 1972.

Lazarus, Arnold. *In the Mind's Eye*. New York, NY: The Guilford Press, 1984.

Leach, Maria, editor. *Standard Dictionary of Folklore, Mythology, and Legend*. New York, NY: Funk & Wagnalls Co., 1950.

Lorusso, Julia, and Joel Glick. *Healing Stoned*. Albuquerque, NM: Brotherhood of Life, 1976.

MacNeill, John, and J.A. Carnoy. *Celtic and Teutonic Religions*. London, England: Catholic Truth Society, 1975.

MacRitchie, David. *Fians, Fairies, and Picts*. London, England: Norwood Editions, 1975.

Malory, Sir Thomas. *Le Morte D'Arthur, Vols. I & II*. New York, NY: Mentor Classics, 1962.

Markale, Jean. *Celtic Civilization*. New York, NY: Gordon & Cremonesi Publishers, 1978.

Markale, Jean. *King Arthur: King of Kings*. New York, NY: Gordon & Cremonesi Publishers, 1977.

Markale, Jean. *Women of the Celts*. New York, NY: Gordon & Cremonesi Publishers, 1975.

Matarasso, P. M. *The Quest of the Holy Grail*. Baltimore, MD: Penguin Books, 1969.

McDowell, C. F. *Leisure Wellness*. Eugene, OR: Sun Moon Press, 1983.

Michell, John. *City of Revelation*. New York, NY: Ballantine Books, 1972.

Michell, John. *The View Over Atlantis*. New York, NY: Ballantine Books, 1969.

Mindell, Arnold. *The Dreambody in Relationships*. New York, NY: Routledge & Kegan Paul, 1987.

Missing Link Newsletter. Starwyn, editor. Chico, CA. Autumn, 1991-Winter, 1993.

Monaghan, Patricia. *The Book of Goddesses and Heroines.* St Paul, MN: Llewellyn Publications, 1990.

Mormouth, Geoffrey. *History of the Kings of Britain.* New York, NY: E.P. Dutton & Co., 1958.

Neil, Fernand. *The Mysteries of Stonehenge.* New York, NY: Avon Books, 1974.

Nesson, Eoin. *The First Book of Irish Myths & Legends.* Cork: Mercier Press, 1966.

Neulinger, John. *The Psychology of Leisure.* Springfield, IL: Charles C. Thomas Publisher, 1974.

Newman, Paul. *The Hill of the Dragon.* London, England: Kingsmead Press, 1976.

Nexxus Newsletter. Newfox, editor. Whitesburg, KY. Spring 1985-Fall, 1988.

Noel, Ruth S. *The Mythology of Middle-Earth.* Boston, MA: Houghton Mifflin Co., 1977.

O'Hettir, Brendon. *A Gaelic Lexicon for Finnegan's Wake.* Berkeley, CA: University of California Press, 1967.

O'Siochfiiradh, Michael. *Irish-English Dictionary.* London, England: Talbot Press, 1958.

Paul, Jordan, and Margaret Paul. *Do I Have To Give Up Me To Be Loved by You?* Minneapolis, MN: CompCare Publishers, 1983.

Pepper, Elizabeth, and John Wilcock. *Magical and Mystical Sites: Europe and the British Isles.* New York, NY: Harper and Row, 1977.

Phillips, Guy Ragland. *Brigantia, A Mysteriography.* London, England: Routledge & Kegan Paul Ltds., 1976.

Piggott, Stuart. *The Druids.* London, England: Thames & Hudson, 1976.

Powell, T.G.E. *The Celts.* New York, NY: Frederick Praeger, Inc., 1975.

Pyle, Howard. *The Story of King Arthur and His Knights.* New York, NY: Dover Publications, 1965.

Raftery, Joseph. *Prehistoric Ireland.* London, England: B.T. Batsford, Ltd., 1951.

Raglan, Lord. *The Hero.* New York, NY: Vintage Books, 1977.

Rahner, Hugo. *Man at Play.* New York, NY: Herder and Herder, 1972.

Ravenwolf, Silver. *To Ride a Silver Broomstick.* St. Paul, MN: Llewellyn Publications, 1993.

Rees, Alwyn and Brinley. *Celtic Heritage, Ancient Tradition in Ireland and Wales.* New York, NY: Grove Press, 1978.

Rhys, John, M. A. *Celtic Folklore, Welsh and Manx.* New York, NY: Benjamin Blom, Inc., 1972.

Rolleston, T. W. *The High Deeds of Finn and Other Bardic Romances of Ancient Ireland.* New York, NY: Lemma Publishing, 1973.

Ross, Anne. *Pagan Celtic Britain.* New York, NY: Columbia University Press, 1967.

Rossi, Ernest L. *The Psychobiology of Mind-Body Healing.* New York, NY: W. W. Norton and Company, 1986.

Rutherford, Ward. *The Druids and Their Heritage.* New York, NY: Gordon & Cremonesi Publishers, 1978.

Ryan, R. S., and J. W. Travis. *Wellness Workbook.* Berkeley, CA: Ten Speed Press, 1981.

Sharkey, John. *Celtic Mysteries.* New York, NY: Avon Books, 1975.

Sharp, William. *The Winged Destiny: Studies in the Spiritual History of the Gael.* New York, NY: Lemma Press, 1975.

Smith, Sir William. *Smaller Classical Dictionary.* New York, NY: E. P. Dutton, 1958.

Spence, Lewis. *The History and Origins of Druidism*. New York, NY: Samuel Weiser, Inc., 1971.

—— *The Magic Arts in Celtic Britain*. New York, NY: Samuel Weiser, Inc., 1970.

—— *The Mysteries of Britain: Secret Rites and Traditions of Ancient Britain Restored*. New York, NY: Samuel Weiser, Inc., 1970.

Squire, Charles. *Celtic Myth and Legend*. Hollywood, CA: Newcastle Publishing Co., 1975.

—— *The Mythology of Ancient Britain and Ireland*. London, England: Follcroft Library, 1975.

Stephens, James. *Irish Fairy Tales*. New York, NY: Collier Books, 1962.

Stewart, C. Nelson. *Gemstones of the Seven Rays*. Mokelumne Hill, CA: Health Research, 1975.

Stewart, R. J. *Celtic Gods, Celtic Goddesses*. New York, NY: Sterling Publishing Co., 1990.

Stone, Brian, translator. *Sir Gawain and the Green Knight*. Baltimore, MD: Penguin Books, Ltd., 1972.

Stone, Merlin. *When God Was a Woman*. New York, NY: Harcourt Brace Javanovich, 1976.

Straus, Roger A. *Strategic Self-Hypnosis*. New York, NY: Prentice Hall Press, 1982.

Taunt, Henry W. *The Rollright Stones; the Stonehenge of Oxfordshire*. Oxford, England: Henry W. Taunt & Co., 1975.

Terry, Patricia, editor. *Poems of the Vikings: the Elder Edda*. New York, NY: Bobbs-Merrill Co., Inc., 1969.

Thorsson, Edred. *Futhark: A Handbook of Rune Magic*. York Beach, ME: Samuel Weiser, Inc., 1984.

Von Strassburg, Gottfried. *Tristan*. Baltimore, MD: Penguin Books, 1960.

Watkins, Alfred. *The Old Straight Track: Its Mounds, Beacons, Moats, Sites, and Markstones*. New York, NY: Ballantine Books, 1973.

Wilcock, John. *A Guide to Occult Britain: The Quest for Magic in Pagan Britain.* London, England: Sidgwick and Jackson, 1976.

Wilde, Lady. *Ancient Legends, Mystic Charms and Superstitions of Ireland.* New York, NY: Lemma Publishing, 1973.

Wilde, Stuart. *The Force.* Taos, NM: Wisdom Books, Inc., 1984.

Yeats, W.B. *The Celtic Twilight.* New York, NY: Signet Books, 1962.

—— *Collected Poems.* New York, NY: MacMillan & Co., 1956.

—— Editor. *Irish Folk Stories and Fairy Tales.* New York, NY: Grosset and Dunlap, 1974.

—— *Mythologies.* New York, NY: Collier Books, 1969.

—— *A Vision.* New York: MacMillan & Co., 1961.

Zerin, Edward Ph.D., and Marjory Zerin, Ph.D. *The "Q" Model for the Effective Management of Personal Stress.* New York, NY: Gardner Press, Inc., 1986.

ℐ Index ℒ

STAY IN TOUCH

On the following pages you will find listed, with their current prices, some of the books now available on related subjects. Your book dealer stocks most of these and will stock new titles in the Llewellyn series as they become available. We urge your patronage.

To obtain our full catalog, to keep informed about new titles as they are released and to benefit from informative articles and helpful news, you are invited to write for our bi-monthly news magazine/catalog, *Llewellyn's New Worlds of Mind and Spirit*. A sample copy is free, and it will continue coming to you at no cost as long as you are an active mail customer. Or you may subscribe for just $10.00 in U.S.A. and Canada ($20.00 overseas, first class mail). Many bookstores also have *New Worlds* available to their customers. Ask for it.

Llewellyn's New Worlds of Mind and Spirit
P.O. Box 64383-386, St. Paul, MN 55164-0383, U.S.A.

* * *

TO ORDER BOOKS AND TAPES

If your book dealer does not have the books described on the following pages readily available, you may order them direct from the publisher by sending full price in U.S. funds, plus $3.00 for postage and handling for orders *under* $10.00; $4.00 for orders *over* $10.00. There are no postage and handling charges for orders over $50.00. Postage and handling rates are subject to change. UPS Delivery: We ship UPS whenever possible. Delivery guaranteed. Provide your street address as UPS does not deliver to P.O. Boxes. UPS to Canada requires a $50.00 minimum order. Allow 4-6 weeks for delivery. Orders outside the U.S.A. and Canada: Airmail—add retail price of book; add $5.00 for each non-book item (tapes, etc.); add $1.00 per item for surface mail.

FOR GROUP STUDY AND PURCHASE

Our Special Quantity Price for a minimum order of five copies of *Greenfire* is $44.85 cash-with-order. This price includes postage and handling within the U.S. Minnesota residents must add 6.5% sales tax. For additional quantities, please order in multiples of five. For Canadian and foreign orders, add postage and handling charges as above. Credit card (VISA, MasterCard, American Express) orders are accepted. Charge card orders only ($15.00 minimum order) may be phoned in free within the U.S.A. or Canada by dialing 1-800-THE-MOON. For customer service, call 1-612-291-1970. Mail orders to:

LLEWELLYN PUBLICATIONS
P.O. Box 64383-386, St. Paul, MN 55164-0383, U.S.A.
Prices subject to change without notice.

THE SACRED MARRIAGE
**Honoring the God and Goddess within
Each Other**
by Lira Silbury

Is your relationship with your partner everything
you hoped it would be? Do you see your partner
as a living manifestation of the Divine—and your
sexual union as a gift to and from the Goddess
and God? Or are you still trapped in old, unful-
filling relationship patterns?

The Sacred Marriage can help you transform every aspect of your relationship from the mundane to the exalted. In this book, you will learn
how—within the foundation of Wicca—you can build a deeper, more
meaningful relationship through sharing meditation and ritual, dreaming together, celebrating the cycles of life and practicing sacred sexuality. If you haven't yet found the right partner for such a relationship,
you will discover ways to draw him or her to you through visualization,
dream work and prayer. If you are already involved in a fulfilling relationship, this book will teach you more about honoring the Divine
within your partnership, with over a dozen beautiful rituals written
especially for couples, including the powerful "Sacred Marriage" cere-
mony for consecrating a long-term commitment.

1-56718-654-8, 6 x 9, 288 pp., illus., softcover   **$14.95**